WELDER

OBJECTIVE QUESTION ANSWERS

MANOJ DOLE

Digitization is the need of the time. In the future, training in industrial training institutes will need to be conducted using online internet to make training more convenient and easy. E-books containing a set of MCQ questions will be made available to the trainees as they need to be more accustomed to the multiple choice questions MCQ to prepare for the online exams taking place in their industrial training institutes.

With all these factors in mind, Mr. Manoj Madhukar Dole Instructor, Industrial Training Institute, Satara, has written books according to the new annual system and NSQF-5 syllabus. And they've created theoretical mobile apps and blogs to make training easier, and made all these educational materials available for download on the world famous websites Google Play Store, Amazon and Apple Book Store.

The books were published by Hon'ble Joint Director Shri Rajendra Ghume Saheb Regional Office of Vocational Education and Training, Pune on 9/1/2019, at this time Shri Prakash Saigavkar Saheb Principal Government Industrial Training Institute Aundh Pune, Shri Tukaram Misal Saheb Principal Govt. Q. Sanstha Satara, Shri Sachin Dhumal Saheb District Vocational Education and Training Officer Satara, Shri Yatin Pargaonkar Saheb Principal Govt. Q. Sanstha Kolhapur, Shri Vikas Teke Saheb Inspector Vocational Education and Training Regional Office Pune, Palekar Foods Products Pvt. Ltd. Entrepreneurial Chairman of Satara Mr. Nilkanthrao Palekar Saheb, Chairman of Hira Foods Mr. Ibrahim Baba Tamboli Saheb, Mrs. Shalmali Pawar Headmaster Government Technical School Center Satara and other dignitaries were present on the occasion.

Contents

Prologue

Welder is a simple Book for ITI & Engineering Course Welder. It contains objective questions with underlined & bold correct answers MCQ covering all topics including all about gas welding plant and join MS sheet, different type of joints on MS, different types of joints- Fillet (T-joint, lap & Corner), Butt (Square & V), oxy- acetylene cutting plant and perform different cutting operations on MS plate, welding in different types of MS pipe joints by Gas welding (OAW), types of MS pipe joints – Butt, Elbow, T-joint, angle (45 Degree) joint, flange joint, SMAW machine and perform welding in different types of MS pipe joints by SMAW, Dye penetration test, Magnetic particle test, Nick break test, Free band test, Fillet fracture test, Aluminium & MS pipe joint by GTAW, Plasma Arc cutting machine and cut ferrous & non-ferrous metals, resistance spot welding machine, brazing operation, Cast Iron machine parts Hard facing of alloy steel components and lots more.

We add new question answers with each new version. Please email us in case of any errors/omissions. This is arguably the largest and best e-Book for All engineering multiple choice questions and answers.

As a student you can use it for your exam prep. This e-Book is also useful for professors to refresh material.

Foreword

Vocational education and training is imparted through the Department of Vocational Education and Training through the Department of Business Education and Business Practical to supply multi-skilled artisans in line with the rapidly growing demand in the industrial sector in the 21st century. All the occupations within the institutions are important, as the trainees from these occupations develop multi-skills as per the demands of the industry.

with the noble intention of making available MCQ e-books suitable for all businesses, considering that all the examinations in all the industries in the industrial sector are conducted online and include MCQ method questions. Mr. Manoj Madhukar Dole has written a very good e-book on MCQ method as per the new annual syllabus. This e-book will definitely be a guide for all the trainees, trainee candidates, training instructors and others concerned.

The author of the book is Mr. Manoj Madhukar Dole, Instructor Gov. ITI Satara has 17 years of training experience. Written as a new annual pattern, this e-book incorporates modern digital QR Code technology to understand the layout, simple language, and simple syntax, diagrams and videos for each subject. So I am sure that this e-book will definitely be useful for in-depth study and exam practice. The work they have done is certainly commendable.

Mr. Tukaram Misal
Principal Government Industrial Training Institute Satara.

Preface

DGET New Delhi and CSTARI Kolkata have been implementing an annual pattern for all businesses in ITI since the August 2018 session. The examination system will also be changed and it will be online from this year and since all the questions are of Objective Type (MCQ), the trainees are in dire need of in-depth study. It is with this in mind that we are delighted to present the books based on the old NIMI pattern and a complete overview of the new annual pattern, and we hope that these books will be a guide for all business directors and trainees. Is.

For writing these books, Johar Awate Saheb, Principal of ITI Akluj. Former Principal of ITI Satara Saigavkar Saheb, Assistant Director Shri Chandrakant Dhekne Saheb Regional Office of Vocational Education and Training, Pune, District Vocational Education and Training Officer Sachin Dhumal Saheb and Headmaster Government Technical School Kendra Shalmali Pawar Madam and son Adhiraj Dole, mother Kusum Dole, I am very grateful to my father Madhukar Dole and wife Ashwini Dole for their special guidance and cooperation from time to time.

Also, in a very short period of time, the book was reviewed by Shri Rajendra Ghume Saheb, Joint Director, Vocational Education and Training Regional Office, Pune, for his invaluable time in publishing the book. I am sincerely grateful for their feedback.

I am grateful to the Instructor of ITI Satara for there continuous support from the very beginning of writing the book.

From this book, I consider myself blessed to have shared my thoughts on e-learning with you. I will not claim that this book is perfect, because considering the perfection, this book is an attempt and is in its infancy. They will be valuable for improvement if they are tested and suggested.

Manoj Dole
Dated 9/1/2019

Acknowledgements

The industrial training and theoretical examination system of our industrial training institutes and these changes have been accepted by the craft instructors and the trainees. Theoretical examinations conducted in your industrial training institutes are also conducted online. Since these examinations are of multiple choice MCQ method, the trainees will need to get more practice of such questions.

With all these considerations in mind, Mr. Manoj Madhukar, Director, Dole Crafts, Katari Industrial Training Institute, Satara, has done a thorough study and with his diligent work and added his keen intellect, according to the new annual system and NSQF-5 syllabus, e-book of Katari and other machine trades. -Book) and they have created mobile apps and blogs on theoretical topics to make training easier and have made all these educational materials available for download on the world famous websites Google Play Store, Amazon and Apple Book Store. Training has been made easier by creating a print version and using advanced techniques like QR Code.

All these educational materials will definitely be a guide for all the trainees for in-depth study and for the craft instructors and other concerned who are imparting vocational training.

CHAPTER ONE

Welder MCQ Drawing

Online Test Exam
ITI Books
CNC Course
AutoCAD CAM
JOB & Apprentice
Online Theory
Computer Course
Trading Course
Web Designing
MSCIT Course
Shopping Business
Internet Business
Remotasks Course
Online Services
Top Sportsmans
Indian Army
Freedom Fighters
Top Scientists
Social Reformers
Motivational Speaker
Top Richest People
Join WhatsApp Group
Join Facebook Group
Like Facebook Page
PAN / Adhar / Licence
Passport

Fire extinguisher

Calliper

Hacksaw frame

Universal surface guage

Hammer

Centre punch

Bench vice

Files

Scraper

Surface Plate

Outside Micrometer

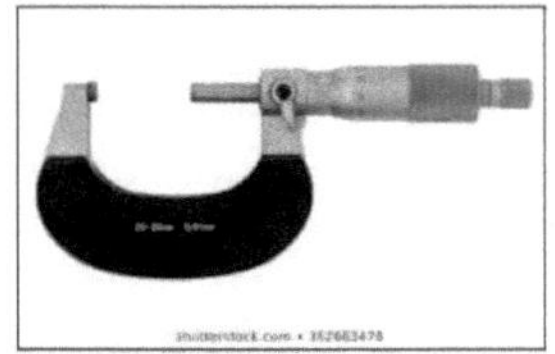

Micrometer

Depth micrometer

Vernier Calliper

Vernier bevel protractor

Drilling

Reamer

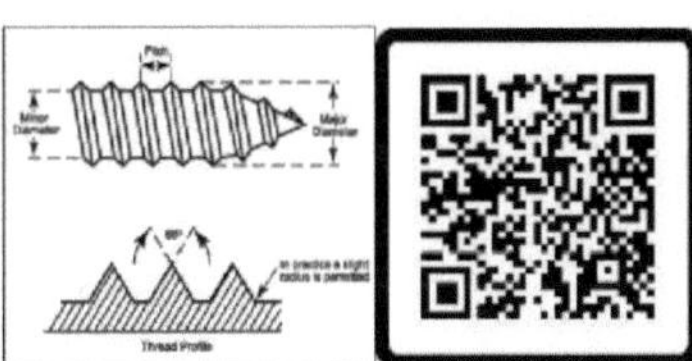

Thread

Tap Die

Grinding Wheel

Tap Die

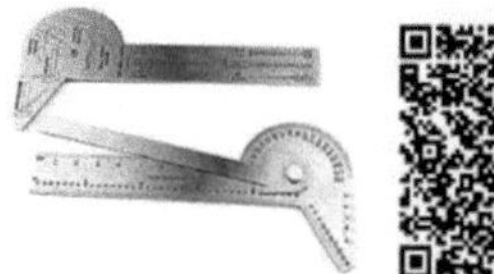

Centre gauge

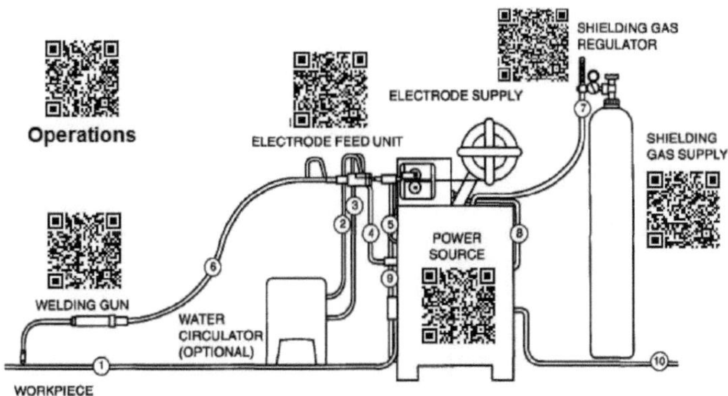

Gas Metal Arc Welding

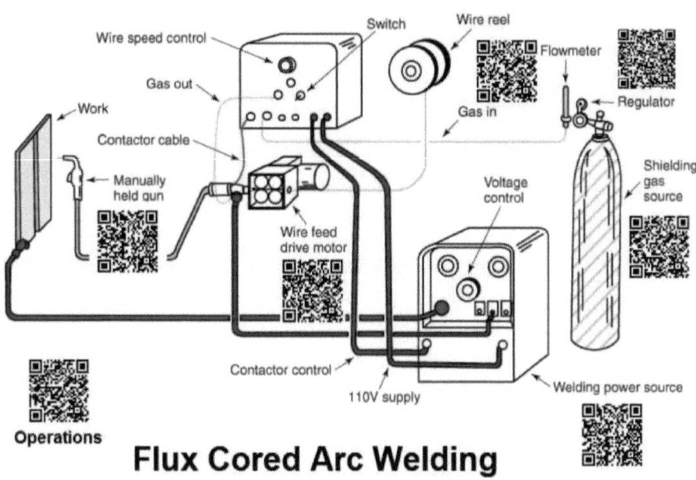

Flux Cored Arc Welding

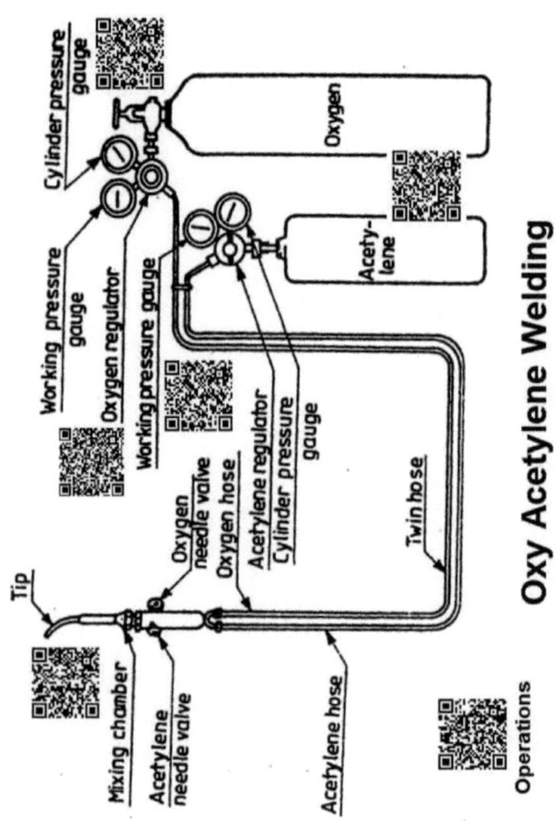

Oxy Acetylene Welding

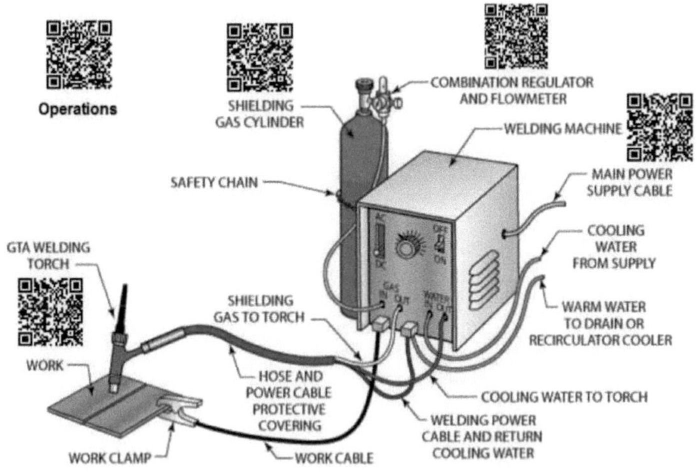

GTAW EQUIPMENT
(GAS TUNGSTEN ARC WELDING)

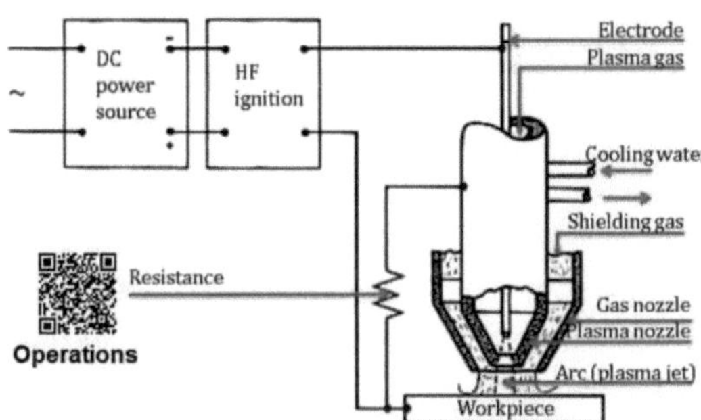

Plasma Transferred Arc Welding

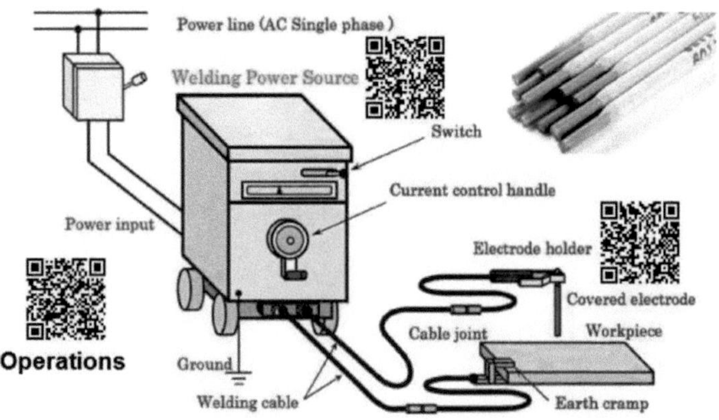

Shielded Metal Arc Welding

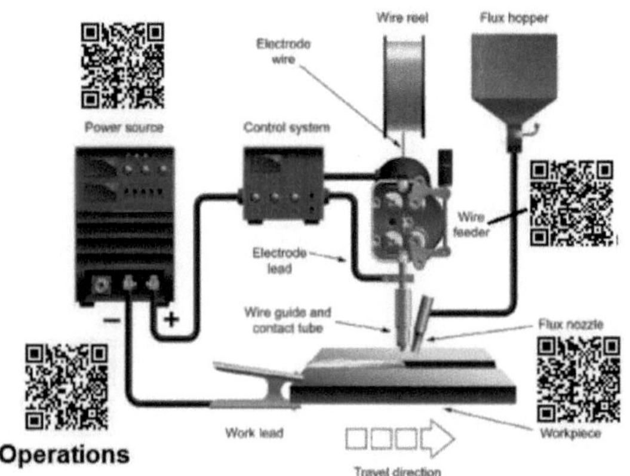

Submerged Arc Welding

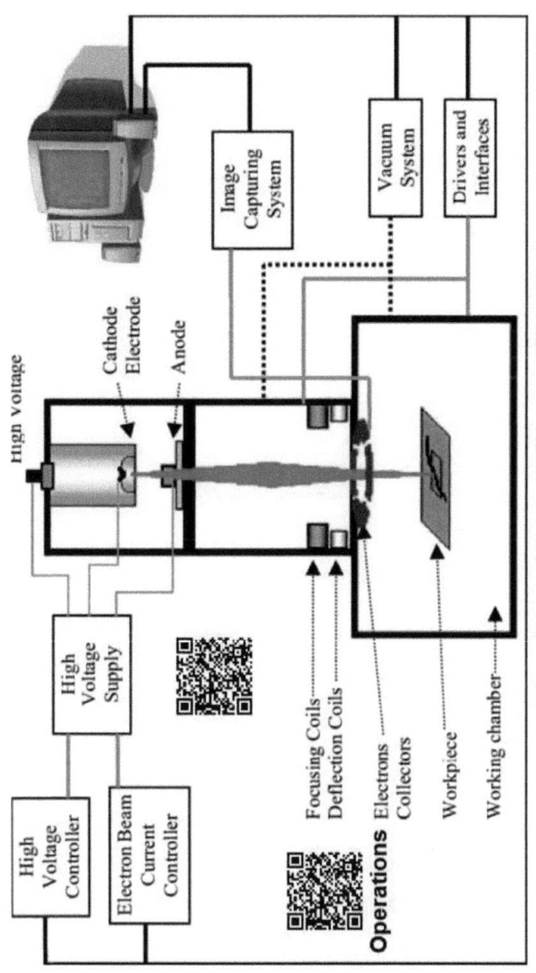
High Voltage
Cathode Electrode
Anode
High Voltage Supply
High Voltage Controller
Electron Beam Current Controller
Image Capturing System
Vacuum System
Drivers and Interfaces
Operations
Focusing Coils
Deflection Coils
Electrons Collectors
Workpiece
Working chamber
Electron Energy Beam Welding

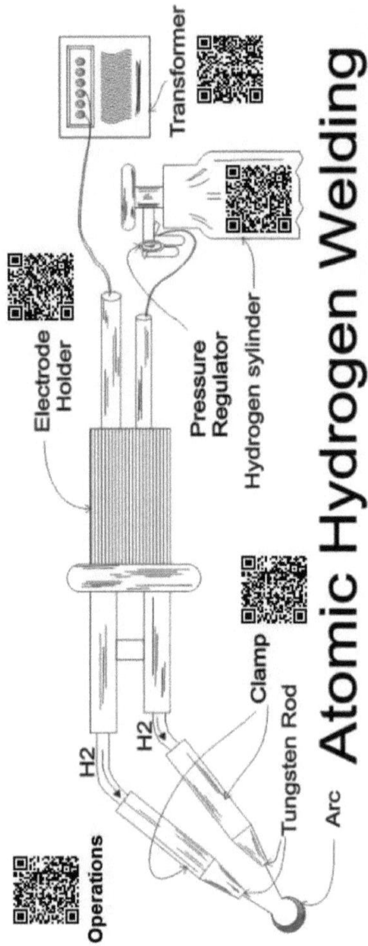
Transformer
Electrode Holder
Pressure Regulator
Hydrogen sylinder
Operations
H2
H2
Clamp
Tungsten Rod
Arc
Atomic Hydrogen Welding

nibbling machine

slant notch

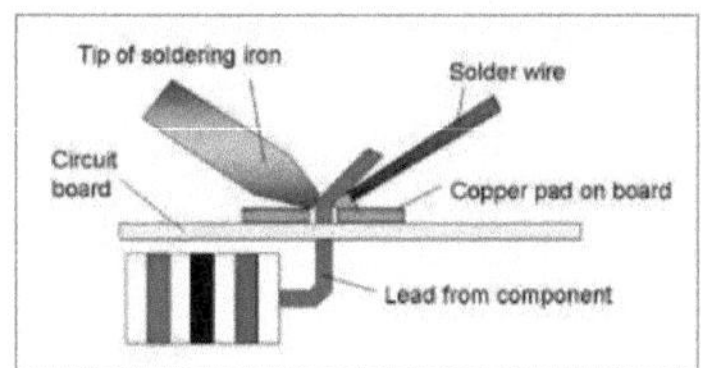

soldering

acytiline gas purifier

hydraulic back pressure valve

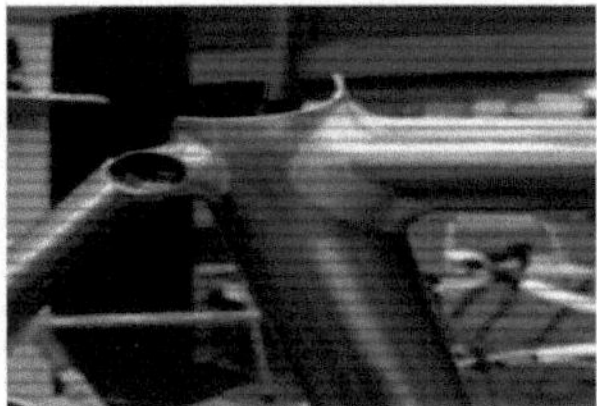

bronze welding

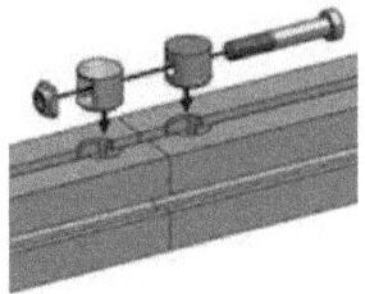

aluminium butt joint

coated electrodes

dc welding generator

nick break test

pipe welding

Figure 1 The two basic types of weld

welding joints

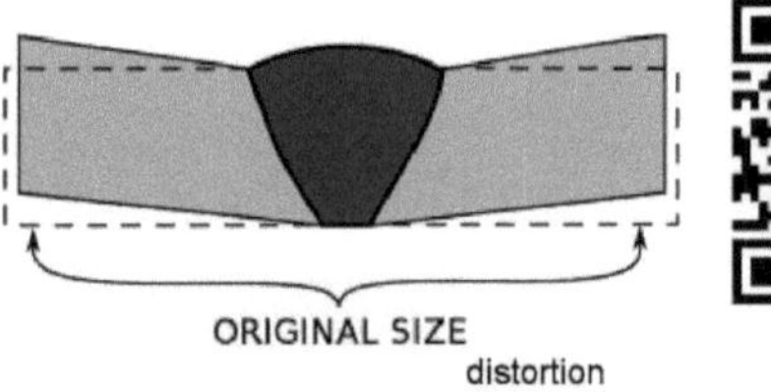

distortion

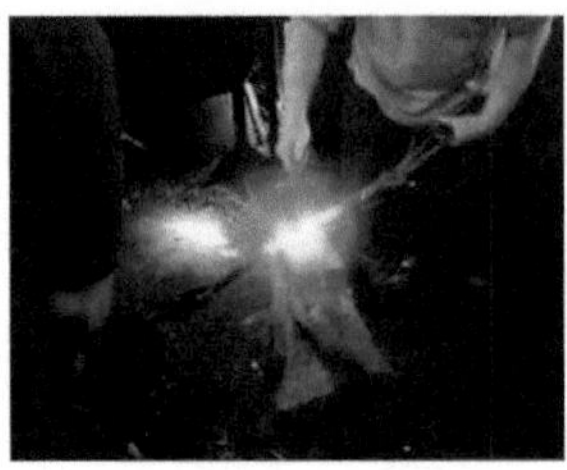

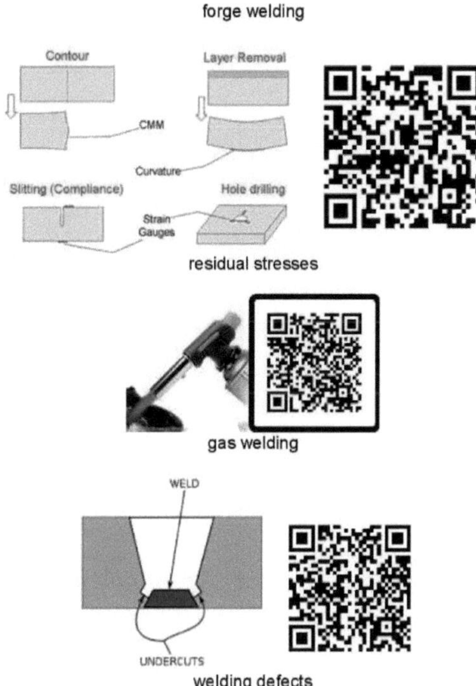

forge welding

residual stresses

gas welding

welding defects

CHAPTER TWO

Welder MCQ

1] Which one is a workshop safety?

A] Keep shop floor clean and free from grease, oil or other slippery materials

B] Stop the machine before changing the speed

C] Don't use cracked or chipped tools

D] Don't try to stop a running machine with hand

2] In Personal Protect Equipment (PPE] HELMET is used to

A] protect head

B] Protect eyes

C] Protect hands

D] Protect ears

3] Which of the following belongs to general safety?

A Have a worker in good attitude

B] The work clean and clear

C] Concentrate on your work

D] Keep the floor and gangways clean and clear

4] While grinding, which is used to protect the eyes?

A] Dark green glass

B] Mask

C] Sun glasses

D] Safety goggles

5] Which of the following is done for machine safety?

A] Check the oil level before starting the machine

B] Do things in a methodical way

C] Keep the floor and gangways clean and clear

D] Don't use dies and scarves

6] In Personal Protect Equipment (PPE], 'sleeves' is used to protect ----------

A] Face
B] Eyes
C] Ears
D] Hands
7] ABC stands for --------------
A] Automatic Breathing Control
B] Automatic Blood Control
C] Airway Breathing Circulation
D] Automatic Blood Circulation
8] Fire & FIRE EXTINGUISHERS

Fire extinguisher

9] To put off"Class B" fire, the types of fire extinguisher used is ....
A] dry power
B] Carbon dioxide
C] Jet of water
D] Foam type
10] Which type of fire extinguisher is used to put off general fire?
A] Water type Extinguisher
B] Foam type Extinguisher
C] Dry chemical powder Extinguisher
D] Carbon dioxide (C02] Extinguisher
11] In case of bleeding, take treatment Of
D] cold 3" and rest
A] spray cold water
B] Bandage immediately -----.
B] Enquire about the accident thought treatment

12] in case of an accident, the victim should im

A] Asked to take rest

C] Attended immediately

D] leave him

13] First aid is given to an injured or ill person primarily....

A] Save life

B] Prevent further deterioration of the muff's

C] Give best possible comfort

D] All of these

14] Colour code for Bins for waste paper segregation is -----

A] blue Colour

B] Yellow Colour

C] Red Colour

D] Green Colour

15] In Japanese Seiko stands for --------------

A] Shine

B] Sort

C] Standardize

D] Sustain

16] Benefit of SS system is ------

A] Increase in productivity

B] Increase in quality

C] Reduction in wastage of time

D] All of these

17] Safety is -----------

A] nobody's business

B] every bodise business

C] Some bodies business

D] The organization business

18] For basic categories of safety signs are available The meaning of"prohibition" sign ----

A] shows it must not be done
B] Shows what must be done
C] Warns the hazard or danger
D] Gives information of safety provision
18] One micrometer (U] is equal to...
A] 0.1mm
B] 0.01mm
C] 0.001mm
D] 0.0001mm
19] The caliper meant for measuring the width of a slot is...
A] Odd leg caliper
B] Outside caliper
C] Jenny caliper
D] Inside calliper

Calliper

20] The size of the dividers are specified by the -----------
A] Total length of legs
B] Distance between the points when fully opened
C] Length of legs without points
D] distance between the pivot and the point
21] The instrument used to mark parallel lines, parallel to the datum edge is -
A] jenny caliper
B] Divider
C] Outside calliper
D] Inside calliper
22] Which one of the following is an indirect measuring tool?
A] Outside caliper
B] Vernier calliper
C] Steel rule

D] Outside micrometer

23] For cutting thin tubing, the most suitable pitch of the hacksaw blade is...

A] 1.8mm

B] 1.4mm

C] 1mm

D] 0.8mm

24] For cutting solid brass, the most suitable pitch of the hacksaw blade is...

A] 1.8mm

B] 1.4mm

C] 1mm

D] 0.8mm

Hacksaw frame

25] A new hacksaw blade after a few strokes becomes loose because of the...

A] Stretching of the blade

B] Wing-nut threads being worn out

C] Wrong pitch of the blade

D] Improper selection of the set of saws.

26] While cutting small diameter pipes, it is advisable to watch regularly and ensure that...

A] The cut is along the curved line

B] More saw teeth are in contract

C] The work is not overheated

D] Proper balancing of hacksaw is maintained

27] The vice clamps are used to...

A] Protect hard jaws

B] Clamp the work pieces rigidly

C] Protect the finished surfaces
D] Prevent the movable jaw being filed
28] The reference surface during marking is provided by the...
A] Surface gauge
B] Workpiece
C] Drawing of the work
D] Marking table surface
29] The size of an engineer's vice is specified by the...
A] Length of the movable jaw
B] Width of the jaws
C] Height of the vice
D] Maximum opening of the jaws
31] Scribers are made of...
A] Mild steel
B] High carbon steel
C] Brass
D] Cast iron
32] Portion of the hammer used for fixing the handle is...
A] Face
B] Peen
C] Cheek
D] Eye hole
33] Weight of the hammer for the marking purpose is...
A] 250g
B] 500g
C] 1 kg
D] 2 kgs

Hammer

34] The size of the dividers are specified by the...
A] Total length of the legs
B] Distance between the points when fully opened
C] Length of legs without the points
D] Distance between the pivot and the point
35] The included angle of the groove of 'V' block is always....
A] 45°
B] 60°
C] 90°
D] 120°
36] 'V' blocks are available in grades of...
A] A & B
B] A,B & C
C] 1,2 & 3
D] 1 & 2
37] 'V' blocks of grade 'B' are made of
A] Cast iron
B] Mild steel
C] Steel
D] Cast steel
38] Name the punch used to locate the centre.
A] Prick punch 30°
B] Prick punch 60°
C] Centre punch
D] Dot punch

Centre punch

39] The point angle of centre punch is --------

A] 30°

B] 50°

c] 900

D] 1200

40] Punches are used for forming ---------of any shape

A] Holes

B] Mining

C] Knurling

D] Reaming

41] Generally the length of the handle of the vice is ----------

A] 1.5 times the normal size of the vice

B] 2.5 times the normal size of the vice

C] 3.5 times the normal size of the vice

D] 4.5 times the normal size of the vice

Bench vice

42] Bench vice spindle is made of ....

A] mild steel

B] Cast iron

C] Tool steel

D] Bronze

43] The convexity of files helps...

A] To file concave surfaces

B] To file convex surfaces

C] To prevent rounding of edges of work

D] The file to become straight when pressure is applied

Files

44] Which file used for filling wood, leather and other soft material? .

A] Single cut file

B] Double cut file

c] Rasp cut file

D] Curved cut file

45] File used is used for ------------

A] Cleaning the work piece

C] Renewing the file teeth

B] cleaning the file teeth

D] Cleaning the chips

46] File card is used to --------

A] Clean the work piece

C] Renew the file teeth

B] Clean the file teeth

47] The point angle of scriber is -----------

A] 30°

B] 60°

C] 5° to 10°

D] 12° to 15°

21] The cutting angle for a straight snip is...

A] 60°

B] 70°

C] 82°

D] 87°

22] Which method of development is used for developing a rectangular tray?

A] triangular method

B] radial line method

C] parallel line method

D] trial and error method

23] What is the profile of the knife cutting edge of the upper blade of the hand level shear?

A] curved

B] straight

C] inclined

D] beveled

24] For what purpose a groover is used in sheet metal work?

A] to make a hem

B] to make grooves

C] to close and lock the seams

D] to strength then the edge of a job

25] Which type of stake is to be selected for making sharp bends, folding of edges of sheet metal?

A] hatchet stake

B] beak iron stake

C] square edge stake

D] tinman's anvil stake

26] Ammonium chloride is used as a flux for soldering...

A] steel

B] aluminium

C] galvanized iron

D] stainless steel

27] Name the tool used to make and finish the leak proof joints of a pipe T joint

A] groover

B] setting hammer

C] creasing hammer

D] round bottom stake

28] Which one of the following metals will not permit X-rays to pass through?

A] stainless steel

B] aluminium

C] lead

D] tin

nibbling machine

29] The frequency of up and down vibration of the cutting edge in a nibbling machine is...

A] 1000 to 1500 times

B] 1500 to 2500 times

C] 2800 to 3000 times

D] 3000 to 3500 times

30] Name the instrument used to check the perpendicularity of the branch pipe with the main pipe of a pipe T joint

A] protractor

B] try square

C] spirit level

D] straight edge

slant notch

31].Which type of notch is used when a single hem meets at right angles?

A] V notch

B] slit notch

C] slant notch

D] square notch

32] To cut out small apertures which punch and die type of machine is used?

A] shear type nibbler

B] punch type nibbler

C] circular cutting machine

D] guillotine shearing machine

33] The overheating of the blow pipe nozzle is to be avoided because it will

A] cause back fire

B] consume more oxygen and acetylene

C] create burn through defect in the joint

D] create undercut defect in the joint

34] State the nozzle size you will select to weld a 3.15mm thick mild steel sheet

A] 3

B.5

C] 7

D] 10

35] The type of flame to be set for welding brass is...

A] air acetylene flame

B] neutral flame

C] oxidizing flame

D] carburizing flame

36] What is the maximum thickness of mild steel sheet recommended for gas welding using lcftward tcchniquc?

A] 12mm

B] 10mm

C] 8mm

D] 5mm

37].The distance between the root and toe of a fillet weld is called...

A] root gap

B] leg length

C] reinforcement

D] throat thickness

38] Name the weld defect which occurs due to improper cleaning of the mild steel sheet edge and surface

A] lack of root penetration

B] burn through

C] undercut

D] porosity

39] Which of the following mechanical properties of metals gives resistance to pulling forces?

A] toughness

B] ductility

C] hardness

D] tensile strength

40] The angle of below pipe to the line of weld in leftward welding technique is...

A] 40 to 50◦

B] 50 to 60◦

C] 60 to 70◦

D] 70 to 80◦

41] The pressure of acetylene gas for gas cutting a 10mm M.S plate is...

A] 0.15 kgf/cm2

B] 0.5 kgf/cm2

C] 1.0 kgf/cm2

D] 1.5 kgf/cm2

42] What size of the cutting nozzle you will select for cutting 10mm thick mild steel?

A] 0.8 mm

B] 1.2 mm

C] 1.6 mm

D] 2.0 mm

43] The angle of filler rod in case of rightward welding technique is...

A] 10 to 20◦

B] 20 to 30◦

C] 30 to 40◦

D] 40 to 50◦

44] One of the advantages of the high pressure system of gas welding is...

A] it is cheaper

B] it is portable
C] it is less dangerous
D] it does not require a skilled welder

soldering

45] Soldering of M.S sheets takes place at a temperature of...
A] 150◦C
B] 250◦C
C] 400◦C
D] 850◦C
46] Forge welding is classified as...
A] fusion welding without pressure
B] fusion welding with pressure
C] non-fusion welding without pressure
D] no-fusion welding with pressure
47] The function of a gas regulator is...
A] get different types of flames
B] mix the gases in the required proportion
C] change the volume of gas flowing to the blow pipe
D] set the working pressure

48] For welding a lap fillet joint in vertical position by gas what should be the angle of below pipe to the line of weld?

A] 30° to 40°

B] 45°to 50°

C] 60° to 70°

D] 75° to 80°

49] Name the defect, in which the weld metal is flowing on to the surface of the base metal without fusing it

A] crater

B] overlap

C] lack of fusion

D] excessive convexity

50] What should be the angle of blow pipe between the two sheets while welding a T joint on 3.15mm M.S> sheet by gas welding?

A] 30°

B] 45°

C] 60°

D] 80°

51] Which metal pipe should NOT be used for passing acetylene gas in order to avoid explosions?

A] galvanized iron

B] stainless steel

C] mild steel

D] cooper

52] he percentage of carbon in acetylene gas is...

A] 99%

B] 92.3%

C] 89.1%

D] 85.3%

53] Acetylene gas contains

A] calcium, carbon and hydrogen

B] calcium and hydrogen

C] calcium, carbon, hydrogen and oxygen

D] carbon and hydrogen

acytiline gas purifier

54] In an acetylene purifier the sulphureted and phosphorated hydrogen are removed by...

A] pumice

B] water

C] filter wool

D] purifying chemicals

55].A hydraulic back pressure valve is used to...

A] increase the pressure of oxygen gas

B] increase the pressure of acetylene gas

C] prevent the danger of back fire

D] decrease the pressure of oxygen

hydraulic back pressure valve

56] The nozzle size required to weld a M.S pipe elbow joint with 3WT to get full depth fusion and good penetration is...

A] 5

B] 7

C] 10

D] 13

57] The selection of nozzle for pipe welding depends upon...

A] groove angle

B] welding position

C] pipe wall thickness

D] diameter of pipe

58] One of the functions of flux in gas welding is...

A] dissolve the metal oxides

B] reduce the melting point of mental

C] increase the flame temperature

D] increase the root penetration

59] The angle of vee groove of a single vee but joint for cast iron welding is...

A] 60°

B] 70°

C] 80°

D] 90°

60] On which of the following factors, the choice of flux for gas welding depend?

A] type of material to be joined

B] type of edge penetration

C] type of fuel gas

D] type of flame used

61].What is the nozzle size required to bronze weld 10mm thick cast iron job?

A] 5

B] 7

C] 10

D] 13

bronze welding

62] State the suitable filler rod for bronze welding of cast iron

A] brass

B] silicon bronze

C] manganese bronze

D] super silicon cast iron

63] In bronze welding of cast iron, the base metal is heated upto a temperature of...

A] 300◦C

B] 650◦C

C] 1000◦C

D] 1300◦C

64] Name the filler rod used for fusion welding of copper

A] manganese bronze rod

B] copper silver alloy rod

C] silicon bronze rod

D] pure copper rod

65] The divergence allowance required for gas welding a 300mm long copper butt joint is...

A] 1 to 2 mm

B] 2 to 3 mm

C] 3 to 4 mm

D] 4 to 5 mm

66] The type of edge preparation done for gas welding a 4mm thick copper butt joint is...

A] single bevel

B] single V

C] double V

D] square

67] The nozzle size used for bronze welding of a 3.15 mm thick copper butt joint is...

A] 5

B] 7

C] 10

D] 13

68] State the filler rod size required for welding a butt joint on 3mm thick brass sheet

A] 1.6 mm

B] 2 mm

C] 2.5 mm

D] 3 mm

69] Name the weld defect which will occur if a No] 3 nozzle is used for welding a 3 mm thick brass sheet

A] undercut

B] burn through

C] porosity

D] lack of penetration

aluminium butt joint

70] The size of nozzle used to gas weld 3.15 mm thick aluminium butt joint is...

A] 13

B] 10

C] 7

D] 5

71] Nozzle size used for welding a 2 mm thick stainless steel sheet as a butt joint is...

A] 2

B] 3

C] 5

D] 7

72] What is the value of preheating temperature for gas welding of aluminium?

A] 100 to 120°C

B] 150 to 180°C

C] 180 to 200°C

D] 210 to 250°C

73] In soldering operation the base metal is...

A] not heated

B] heated to 200°C

C] heated to 650°C

D] heated to red hot condition

74] For welding dissimilar metals, the following property of both the metals should not have wide variations

A] ductility

B] tensile strength

C] thermal expansion

D] wear resistance

75] Name the flux used for brazing of M.S] sheets

A] hydrochloric acid

B] zinc chloride

C] tallow resin

D] borax

76] In progressive gouging to what angle the gouging torch angle is reduced from the starting angle of 30◦?

A] 20 to 25◦

B] 15 to 20◦

C] 10 to 15◦

D] 5 to 10◦

77] The thermit mixture used in thermit welding can be ignited with an initial temperature of..

A] 1500◦C

B] 1200◦C

C] 1000◦C

D] 500◦C

78] Shielded metal arc welding is classified under the process of...

A] electric resistance welding

B] special welding

C] electric arc welding

D] electro gas welding

79] How to specify the size of an electrode holder?

A] by its weight

B] by its shape

C] by its current carrying capacity

D] by the metal used for making it

80] The current set for a 3.15mm medium coated mild steel electrode is...

A] 50 to 80 amp

B] 90 to 120 amp

C] 120 to 150 amp

D] 150 to 170 amp

81] Which method of cleaning you will use to remove oil, grease and paint from the surface of the metals to be welded?

A] filing

B] wire brushing

C] washing with cold water

D] using solvents of diluted hydrochloric acid

82] In the electrode coding ER4211, the third digit of the number 4211 indicates....

A] welding current and voltage condition

B] elongation and impact properties

C] tensile strength of the joint

D] welding position

83] A long arc is used in...

A] welding with a low hydrogen electrode

B] horizontal position

C] plug or slot welding

D] cast iron welding

84] If the travel speed of electrode is high, which type of weld defect you will get on a T fillet joint?

A] overlap

B] slag inclusion

C] excessive reinforcement

D] lack of root penetration

85] Which weld defect occurs on a lap fillet joint due to improper weaving of the electrode in the covering/final run?

A] crack

B] undercut

C] lack of fusion

D] edge of plate melted off

86] A lap fillet weld has uneven bead height] What is the cause for this defect?

A] use of high current

B] low welding travel speed

C] use of wrist movement for the electrode weaving

D] high welding travel speed

87] The coating factor used to make medium coated electrode is...

A] 1.25 to 3

B] 1.4 to 1.5

C] 1.6 to 2.2

D] above 2.2

coated electrodes

88] Which type of coated electrodes are used for general purpose welding and for training purposes in ITIs?

A] basic coated

B] iron powder

C] cellulosic

D] rutile

89] Maintaining a key hole and use of proper root gap in a single V butt joint will ensure...

A] reducing the arc blow effect

B] faster metal deposition

C] proper root penetration

D] proper reinforcement

90] At what angle the electrode is to be held with the bottom surface of the joint in horizontal position?

A] 60◦ to 70◦

B] 70◦ to 80◦

C] 80◦ to 90◦

D] 90◦ to 100◦

91] Upto which temperature a moisture affected (wet) electrode is to be heated for one hour?

A] 50 to 100◦C

B] 110 to 150◦C

C.160 to 200◦C

D] 200 to 250◦C

92] The purpose of presenting the plate while welding a T fillet joint is to...

A] get good root penetration

B] avoid crater defect

C] control distortion

D] control arc blow

93] Lack of penetration in a butt welded joint is due to...

A] too low welding speed

B] short arc length

C] high current

D] low current

94].Which type of distortion can be controlled by presenting of plates to be welded?

A] angular distortion

B] transverse distortion

C] longitudinal distortion

D] distortion due to locked-up stresses

95] What is the percentage carbon present in mild steel?

A] 0.05 to 0.1%

B] 0.15 to 0.3%

C] 0.5 to 0.8%

D] 0.8 to 1.4%

96] If a high carbon steel plate is heated to above its higher critical temperature and then suddenly cooled, it will become...

A] annealed

B] tempered

C] hardened

D] normalized

97] Residual stresses present in a welded job will

A] increase hardness of the weld

B] decrease ductility of the weld

C] crack the joint when load is applied

D] increase the life of a welded joint

98] Which one of the following metal has highest thermal conductivity?

A] zinc

B] copper

C] mild steel

D] aluminium

99] Which one of the following metal has the highest melting temperature?

A] copper

B] tungsten

C] aluminium

D] mild steel

100] Which one of the below given welding machines can be used for both AC and DC welding?

A] engine driven welding generator

B] motor driven welding generator

C] welding transformer

D] welding rectifier

dc welding generator

101] The name of the part in a DC welding generator which converts the AC supply voltage into DC welding output voltage is...

A] armature

B] commutator

C] field coils

D] carbon brushes

102] Which one of the following is the reason for poor fusion of bead with the base metal?

A] electrode travel too slow

B] current too high

C] current too low

D] arc too short

103] Which one of the following defects will occurs if the percentage of phosphorus is more in the base metal?

A] slag inclusion

B] surface crack

C] lack of fusion

D] undercut

104] Which method of test you will use to check a surface crack on a mild steel welded joint at a cheaper cost?

A] X-ray test

B] ultrasonic test

C] visual inspection

D] magnetic particle test

nick break test

105] Which one of the following defects can be tested found by a Nick Break test on T fillet joint?

A] crater cracks

B] surface cracks

C] lack of root penetration

D] insufficient throat thickness

106] Which one of the following metal plates can NOT be joined by projection welding process?

A] tin plates

B] copper plates

C] mild steel plates

D] stainless steel plates

pipe welding

107] In which position of pipe welding, the pipe is fixed and inclined at 45° to both horizontal and vertical plane?

A] 1G

B] 2G

C] 5G

D] 6G

108] The current to be set for welding a pipe butt joint with a 2.5mmØ rutile coated M.S electrode is...

A] 50A to 70A

B] 70A to 80A

C] 80A to 90A

D] 90A to 100A

109] Downhill method of welding of pipe is done while welding

A] a thin walled pipe by rolling

B] a thin walled pipe in fixed position

C] a thick walled pipe by rolling

D] a thick walled pipe in fixed position

110] In which pipe welding position all positional welding is required to be done?

A] 1G (Rolling)

B] 2G

C] 5G

D] 1G (segmental)

111] Which property of cast iron makes it difficult to weld cast iron?

A] high compressive strength

B] hardness and brittleness

C] low melting point

D] low fluidity

112] The type of electrode selected for welding cast iron with mild steel plate is...

A] M.S] electrode

B] <u>bronze electrode</u>

C] low hydrogen electrode

D] stainless steel electrode

113] Name the solution used for cleaning the copper sheets during pickling

A] diluted nitric acid

B] <u>diluted sulphuric acid</u>

C] diluted hydrochloric acid

D] diluted carbon tetra chloride

114] Which type of electrode is used for fusion welding of copper?

A] electrolyte copper

B] copper silicon electrode

C] phosphor bronze electrode

D] <u>deoxidized copper electrode</u>

115] The usual defect which occurs on a weld done by low heat input electrode due to improper cleaning is...

A] undercut

B] <u>porosity</u>

C] overlap

D] crack

welding joints

116] Columbium based stainless steel electrode is used for welding stainless steel joints] The will prevent...

A] Crack in the joint

B] weld decay

C] distortion

D] spatter

117] Porosity in stainless steel weld is due to the use of...

A] short arc

B] less current

C] damp electrode

D] unstabilised electrode

118] Which one of the following is used in the oxy-arc cutting process?

A] flux coated solid electrode

B] bare wire tubular electrode

C] flux coated tubular electrode

D] bare tungsten arc cutting electrode

119] The electrode holder in a carbon arc cutting equipment is made up of...

A] plain carbon steel

B] galvanized iron

C] aluminium

D] copper

121] for making gutters, roof flashing, hoods etc]

A] Galvanised iron

B] Stainless steel

C] Copper sheet

D] Metal sheets

122] in dairies] food processing, kitchen ware etc]

A] Galvanised iron

B] Stainless steel

C] Copper sheet

D] Metal sheets

123] for making buckets, heating ducts, cabinets etc]

A] Galvanised iron

B] Stainless steel

C] Copper sheet

D] Metal sheets

124] in canneries and chemical plants Metal sheets

A] Galvanised iron

B] Stainless steel

C] Copper sheet

D] Metal sheets

125] Ammonium chloride is used as a flux for soldering...

A] steel

B] aluminium

C] galvanized iron

D] stainless steel

126] Soldering of M.S sheets takes place at a temperature of...

A] 150◦C

B] 250◦C

C] 400◦C

D] 850◦C

127] In soldering operation the base metal is...

A] not heated

B] heated to 200◦C

C] heated to 650◦C

D] heated to red hot condition

128] Rivets for Joining sheets to thick plates]

A] Countersunk head

B] Flat head

C] Pan head

D] Mushroom

129] Rivets for Joining sheet metal]

A] Countersunk head

B] Flat head

C] Pan head

D] Mushroom

130] Rivets for Heavy fabrication work]

A] Countersunk head

B] Flat head

C] Pan head

D] Mushroom

131] Rivets for Reduces the height of rivet head above the meta\ surface

A] Countersunk head

B] Flat head

C] Pan head

D] Mushroom

132] Rivets for commonly used for structural work]

A] Countersunk head

B] Flat head

C] Pan head

D] Snap head

135] Ammonium chloride is used as a flux for soldering...

A] steel

B] aluminium

C] galvanized iron

D] stainless steel

136] Soldering of M.S sheets takes place at a temperature of...

A] 150◦C

B] 250◦C

C] 400◦C

D] 850◦C

137] In soldering operation the base metal is...

A] not heated

B] heated to 200◦C

C] heated to 650◦C

D] heated to red hot condition

138] Soft soldering is done

A] below 450◦ C

B] above 450◦C

C] at 900◦C

D] above 1000◦C

139] Brazing is done

A] at 1900◦C

B] above 450◦C

C] at 1000◦C

D] below 450◦C

140] A brazed joint is

A] weaker than a soldered joint

B] stronger than a solder join

C] stronger than a welded joint

D] weaker than a silver soldered joint

Q 2] ________ is used to protect the eyes and face of a welder from arc radiation and spark during arc welding]

A] Apron

B] Welding hand screen

C] Chipping goggle

D] Safety shoe

Q 3] Which of the following gas does not burn itself but is helpful in combustion?

A] Oxygen

B] Nitrogen

C] Argon

D] None of these

Q 4] The source of heat in electric arc welding is ________

A] Friction

B] thermit

C] gas flame

D] Electricity

Q 5] The source of heat in gas welding is ________

A] voltage

B] thermit

C] gas flame

D] Electricity

Q 6] Which of the following equipment is used in arc welding ?

A] Electrode holder

B] Oxygen gas cylinder

C] Welding blowpipe

D] None of these

Q 7] Which of the following equipment is used in gas welding ?

A] Gas regulator

B] Oxygen gas cylinder

C] Welding blowpipe

D] All of these

Q 8] Which of the following is a metal joining process?

A] Welding

B] Brazing

C] Riveting

D] All of these

Q 9] Which of the following method makes a permanent joint?

A] Welding

B] Riveting

C] Bolting

D] None of these

Q 10] Identify the given equipment]

A] Tip cleaner

B] Welding screen

C] Electrode holder

D] None of these

Q 11] Which of the following statement is true about neutral flame?\
A] Complete combustion takes place in this flame]
B] For welding mild steel neutral flame is used]
C] There are two zones in neutral flame]
D] <u>All of these</u>
Q 12] Which gas is produced when reacting with calcium carbide water?
A] <u>Acetylene</u>
B] Oxygen
C] Nitrogen
D] Argon
Q 13] Which type of oxy-acetylene flame is used for welding mild steel?
A] <u>Neutral flame</u>
B] Oxidising flame
C] Carburising flame
D] Acidic flame
Q 14] Which of the following is not a type of oxy-acetylene flame
A] Neutral flame
B] Oxidising flame
C] Carburising flame
D] <u>Acidic flame</u>
Q 15] What is the chemical formula of acetylene gas?
A] CH
B] CH2
C] <u>C2H2</u>
D] None of these
Q 16] Identify the type of oxy-acetylene gas flame shown in the picture]
A] Neutral flame
B] Oxidising flame
C] <u>Carburising flame</u>
D] None of these
Q 17] Oxygen is approximately _____% in the atmosphere]
A] 78
B] 0]03
C] <u>21</u>
D] 7
Q 18] What is the chemical symbol of oxygen gas?
A] C
B] CH

C] N2
D] O2
Q 19] The color of the oxygen gas cylinder is ______]
A] green
B] black
C] red
D] Blue
Q 20] The work of gas regulator is ______]
A] getting different types of flames
B] mixing the mixture of gases into the expected proportion
C] to clean hose pipe
D] setting up the working pressure
Q 21] Nozzle of gas welding blowpipe is made up of which metal?
A] Mild steel
B] Copper
C] Cast iron
D] Tin
Q 22] Identify the equipment shown in the picture]
A] Gas regulator
B] Welding blowpipe
C] Tip cleaner
D] Spark lighter
Q 23] Which of the following is used as a flux in brazing?
A] Borax
B] Boric acid
C] Both borax and boric acid
D] None of these
Q 24] Which of the following flame is suitable for preheating before flame
cutting?
A] Oxidizing flame
B] Neutral flame
C] Carburizing flame
D] none of these
Q 25] What happens if a very little oxygen is supplied in gas cutting?
A] The metal will be cooled down
B] The kerf will be narrow
C] The kerf will be wide

D] The metal will not cut completely

Q 26] Which of the following is a type of manifold system?

A] Portable

B] Stationary

C] Both portable and stationary

D] None of these

Q 27] Identify the welding defect shown in the picture]

A] Overlap

B] Undercut

C] Crack\दरार

D] Lack of fusion

Q 28] Name the gas welding defect in which number of pinholes formed on the surface of deposited metal]

A] Crack

B] Porosity

C] Lack of fusion

D] check and forget method

Q 29] Which of the following equipment is used in oxy-acetylene gas cutting?

A] Spark lighter

B] Tip cleaner

C] Cutting torch

D] All of these

Q 30] Which of the following metal can be cut by oxy acetylene gas cutting process?

A] Mild steel

B] Aluminium

C] Copper

D] All of these

Q 31] ______________ is the property of substance to oppose the flow of electric current passing through it]\ ______________

A] Electric current

B] Electric resistance

C] Conductivity

D] Voltage

Q 32] If V= voltage, I= current and R is the resistance of an electrical circuit then which of the following relation is correct according to Ohm's law?

A] I=VR
B] R=VI
C] V=IR
D] None of these
Q 33] Which of the following is a conductor of electricity?
A] Wood
B] Glass
C] Copper
D] All of these
Q 34] Electric arc welding is also called as________]
A] MAG
B] MIG
C] MMAW
D] TIG
Q 35] Which one of the following can be used as a power source in arc welding?
A] AC welding transformer
B] DC motor generator
C] Rectifier set
D] All of these
Q 36] What type of transformer is used in arc welding?
A] Step-up
B] Neutral
C] Step-down
D] None of these
Q 37] Which of the following is a part of DC welding generator?
A] Armature
B] Commutator
C] Yoke
D] All of these
Q 38] Which of the following is a disadvantage of DC welding?
A] Higher initial cost
B] Higher operating cost
C] Higher maintenance cost
D] All of these
Q 40] A complete welding symbol consists which of the following element?
A] Welding elementary symbol

B] Supplementary symbol
C] Reference line
D] All of these
Q 41] Which type of arc length is used in plug and slot welding?
A] Normal Arc length
B] Long Arc length
C] Short Arc length
D] Zero Arc length
Q 42] _______ arc is used for positional welding]
A] Normal
B] Long
C] Short
D] Zero
Q 43] Which of the following welding position is the easiest to welding?
A] overhead
B] Vertical
C] Flat
D] Horizontal
Q 44] In straight polarity the electrode is connected to the ________ terminal of electric power source]
A] neutral
B] positive
C] both neutral and positive
D] Negative
Q 45] Which of the following is not an electric welding process?
A] Electric arc welding
B] Gas metal arc welding
C] Oxy-acetylene gas welding
D] None of these
Q 46] Brass is an alloy of copper and ________
A] aluminium
B] zinc
C] tin
D] Steel
Q 47] Identify the welding defect shown in the picture]
A] Overlap
B] Undercut
C] Crack

D] Lack of fusion

Q 48] Which of the following is an external arc welding defect?

A] Undercut

B] Overlap

C] Spatter

D] All of these

Q 49] Which of the following is another name of gas metal arc welding ?

A] MIG welding

B] Plasma welding

C] TIG welding

D] None of these

Q 50] Which of the following is a basic equipment for a gas metal arc welding setup?

A] Welding power source

B] Wire feeder

C] Welding gun

D] All of these

Q 51] Which of the following is an advantage of gas metal arc welding?

A] Thick and thin material can be welded

B] Welding in all positions can be done

C] Deposition rate is high

D] All of these

Q 52] Identify the welding defect shown in the picture]

A] Overlap

B] Undercut

C] Porosity

D] Lack of fusion

Q 53] What does FCAW stands for?

A] Flux Cored Arc Welding

B] Full Cored Arc Welding

C] Flux Cored Automatic Welding

D] None of these

Q 54] Which of the following inert gas is used in MIG welding?

A] Argon

B] Xenon

C] Oxygen

D] Nitrogen

Q 55] Which part of Gas metal arc welding set controls the speed of wire electrode and provide the path for welding current and gas flow?

A] Welding power source

B] Wire feeder

C] Welding gun

D] Shielding gas cylinder

Q 56] The electrode used in GMAW is in ______ form]

A] rod

B] spring

C] coil

D] Wire

Q 57] Which of the following is a defect in GMAW?

A] Undercut

B] Spatter

C] Crack

D] All of these

Q 58] GTAW is also known as_______ welding]

A] TIG

B] MIG

C] MAG

D] MMAW

Q 59] What is the purpose of the high frequency unit available in TIG welding machine?

A] Starting the arc

B] Increasing Arc Voltag

C] Reducing welding current

D] None of these

Q 60] Name the welding process shown in the picture]

A] TIG

B] MIG

C] MAG

D] MMAW

Q 61] In straight polarity of TIG welding , ______% of the heat goes to the

electrode end]

A] 30

B] 50

C] 70

D] 100

Q 62] The electrode in TIG welding is made of ________]

A] Copper

B] steel

C] tungsten

D] Zinc

Q 63] Name that welding process that maintains electric arc between nonconsumable

tungsten electrode and the base metal?

A] TIG

B] MIG

C] MAG

D] MMAW

Q 64] Which of the following is a part of gas tungsten arc welding torch?

A] Collet

B] Nozzle

C] Collet holder

D] All of these

Q 65] There is a standard colour indication for tungsten electrodes] Pure tungsten is marked with _________ colour]

A] green

B] black

C] red

D] Blue

Q 66] The color of the argon gas cylinder is _____]

A] green

B] black

C] red

D] peacock blue

Q 67] Identify the welding joint shown in the picture]

A] Tee joint

B] Corner joint

C] Butt joint

D] Lap joint

Q 68] Which of the following is an advantage of Pulsed TIG welding?

A] Less distortion

B] Better penetration with less heat

C] Both less distortion and better penetration with less heat

D] None of these

Q 69] What is the name of the defect in which the weld metal did not melt

with base metal in TIG welding process?

A] Porosity

B] Lack of fusion

C] Undercut

D] Crack

Q 70] Name the welding process shown in the picture]

A] Electron beam welding

B] Plasma welding

C] Submerged arc welding

D] Thermit welding

Q 71] Which type of flux is used in submerged arc welding?

A] Granular

B] Powder

C] Paste

D] No flux is used

Q 72] The electrode used in submerged arc welding is in ______ form]

A] rod

B] spring

C] coil

D] Wire

Q 73] Which of the following is a part of submerged arc welding machine?

A] Flux hopper

B] Wire feeder

C] Power source

D] All of these

Q 74] Which of the following is a type of resistance welding process?

A] Friction welding

B] Electroslag welding

C] Seam welding

D] None of these

Q 75] In which of the following welding process pressure is applied on the

joint?

A] Resistance welding

B] Gas metal arc welding

C] TIG welding

D] All of these

Q 76] In which of the following welding process electrode is in the form of

rollers?

A] TIG welding

B] Seam welding

C] Spot welding

D] Gas metal arc welding

Q 77] Which of the following is not a type of cast iron?

A] White cast iron

B] Malleable cast iron

C] Ductile cast iron

D] Yellow cast iron

Q 78] Heating the job before welding operation is known as________]

A] hardening

B] post heating

C] pre-heating

D] Quenching

Q 79] An alloy of iron, chromium and nickel is called as _________

A] brass

B] bronze

C] stainless steel

D] Solder

Q 80] Which of the following is an arc cutting and gouging process?

A] Air arc cutting process

B] Plasma arc cutting process

C] Carbon arc cutting process

D] All of these

Q 81] Which of the following welding process can be employed for welding

mild steel?

A] Arc welding

B] Oxy-acetylene gas welding

C] Gas metal arc welding

D] All of these

Q 82] What does W stands for in WPS?

A] Work

B] Worker

C] Welding

D] None of these

Q 83] Test in which, specimen is tested without breaking is called______]

A] Destructive test

B] Non- Destructive test

C] Tensile strength test

D] Semi destructive test

Q 84] Which of the following is a non destructive test?

A] Ultrasonic test

B] Magnetic particle test

C] Radiographic test

D] All of these

Q 85] Name the equipment given below]

A] Tip cleaner

B] Spark lighter

C] Weld gauge

D] None of these

Q 86] What does R stands for, in PQR?

A] Read

B] Run

C] Record

D] None of these

Q 87] Which of the following is not an arc welding process?

A] Electric arc welding

B] Gas metal arc welding

C] Resistance welding

D] None of these

Q 88] Which of the following is welding safety apparel?

A] Welding apron

B] Welding hand gloves

C] Hand sleeve

D] All of these

Q 89] Identify the tool shown in the picture]

A] Tong

B] Chipping hammer

C] Wire brush

D] Tip cleaner

Q 90] As the thickness of the material to be welded by arc welding increases, the welding current required

A] Increases

B] Decreases

C] Remains the same

D] May increase or decrease

Q 91] The type of current preferred for welding non-ferrous metal is

A] High frequency alternating current

B] Low frequency alternating current

C] Direct current

D] No preference

Q 92] The material used for coating of electrodes is called

A] Slag

B] Flux

C] Sticker

D] Binder

Q 93] Is it OK to wear nylon clothing when doing welding?

A] No, it causes too much sweating

B] No, it can catch fire easily

C] It's fine, you can wear it

D] No, because it can create static electricity and cause shock

Q 94] Acetylene can be prepared by chemical reaction between

A] Water and calcium carbide

B] Water and calcium carbonate

C] Hydrogen and calcium carbide

D] Hydrogen and calcium carbonate

Q 95] How is the size of an arc welding electrode specified?

A] By its weight

B] By the metal it is required to weld

C] By its current carrying capacity

D] By its overall diameter

Q 96] Which material can be best cut by oxy-acetylene cutting?

A] Brass

B] Cast iron

C] Mild steel

D] Aluminium

Q 97] The gas which is supporter of combustion is

A] Oxygen
B] Hydrogen
C] Carbon dioxide
D] Acetylene
Q 98] The entrapment of gas in the weld causes the defect
A] Lack of fusion
B] Cracks
C] Porosity
D] Slag inclusion
Q 99] As a matter of safety, one should not do arc welding
A] While standing on wet floor
B] In poor lighted area
C] When someone standing nearby
D] In well ventilated confined area
Q 100] What may happen if oil or grease is used on gas regulator?
A] Oil or grease may burn
B] Regulator may burn
C] Cylinder may explode
D] All of these
Q 101] The original metal being joined by welding is called
A] Bare metal
B] Bead metal
C] Base metal
D] Raw metal
Q 102] Which statement is not true about MIG welding?
A] The speed of welding is high
B] There is no slag to be removed
C] The welds produced are sound
D] Electric arc is not visible to the operator
Q 103] In electrode-positive welding , ...of total heat is produced at the electrode]
A] Two-third
B] One-third
C] One-half
D] One-fourth
Q 104] What medium is used to dissolve acetylene?
A] Water
B] Acetone

C] Jelly

D] Calcium hydroxide

Q 105] A cylinder which contains acetylene is painted

A] Bluc

B] Black

C] Maroon

D] Brown

Q 106] The term used to indicate amount of current flowing in a circuit is

called]]]]]]]]

A] Ohm

B] Ampere

C] Farad

D] Volt

Q 107] What should be used to clean the tip orifice of gas cutting torch?

A] Tip cleaner

B] Steel wire

C] Copper wire

D] Small drill

Q 108] Which weld defect can be easily detected by visual examination?

A] Lack of side wall fusion

B] Root defect in a T fillet joint

C] Slag inclusion

D] Misalignment of parts

Q 109] Which one of these metals has the highest thermal conductivity?

A] Aluminium

B] Copper

C] Zinc

D] Steel

distortion

Q 110] Two plates being welded get pulled towards each other and the angle between them changes from the originally set angle] The distortion caused is called

A] Universal distortion

B] Longitudinal distortion

C] Angular distortion

D] Transverse distortion

Q 111] Which testing method can be hazardous to the operator?

A] X - ray test

B] Ultrasonic test

C] Liquid penetrant test

D] Magnetic particle test

Q 112] Which of these is a non-destructive test?

A] Impact test

B] Nick break test

C] Tensile test

D] Hydraulic pressure test

Q 113] The melting point of medium carbon steel is

A] 1510 degree C

B] 1426 degree C

C] 1305 degree C

D] 1082 degree C

Q 114] The last bit of unused electrode is called

A] Waste end

B] Discard end

C] Stub end

D] Little end

Q 115] What is used to conduct current from welding cable to electrode?

A] Earth cable

B] Electrode holder

C] Earth clamp

D] Cable lug

Q 116] What is the open circuit voltage of a welding transformer?

A] 90 V

B] 110 V

C] 130 V

D] 150 V

Q 117] The welding machine which can supply both AC and DC]

A] Engine driven welding generator

B] Motor driven welding generator

C] Welding transformer

D] Welding rectifier

Q 118] For gas cutting of 6 mm thick mild steel plate, what should be the size of the nozzle?

A] 0]4 mm

B] 0]6 mm

C] 0]8 mm

D] 1]0 mm

Q 119] The function of gas regulator is ....

A] To mix gases in required proportion

B] To set the working pressure

C] To get different types of flames

D] To change the volume of gas flowing through the blowpipe

Q 120] What edge preparation should be used for welding of 12 mm thick

MS plate?

A] Single

B] Double

C] Single

D] No bevelling

Q 121] It is easiest to weld in ....

A] Horizontal position

B] Vertical position

C] Overhead position

D] Downhand position

Q 122] Which fuel gas gives maximum flame temperature?

A] Acetylene

B] Coal gas

C] Hydrogen

D] Liquid petroleum gas

Q 123] Spatter during arc welding happens due to ....

A] High welding current

B] Use of damp electrodes

C] Use of short arc

D] Arc blow

Q 124] What is the purpose of water supply in TIG welding?

A] Cool the job

B] Wash the torch

C] Avoid distortion

D] Cool the torch

Q 125] The distance from work surface to the top of the weld bead is called ....

A] Bead width

B] Reinforcement

C] Penetration

D] Fusion zone

Q 126] If the weld does not combine with another weld or the base metal,

it is referred to as ....

A] Incomplete fusion

B] Incomplete bonding

C] Incomplete penetration

D] Incomplete inclusion

Q 127] Vapours of lead, zinc and cadmium ....

A] Can be ignored

B] Are highly flammable

C] Are hazardous

D] May cause slag inclusion

Q 128] Normally acetylene should be discharged from a cylinder at a rate which will empty it in not less than ....

A] 2 hours

B] 5 hours

C] 8 hours

D] 10 hours

Q 129] The type of electrodes which pick up moisture easily is

A] Acidic coated electrodes

B] Basic coated electrodes

C] Rutile coated electrodes

D] Titanium coated electrodes

Q 1] Identify the welding joint shown in the picture]

A] Tee joint

B] Corner joint

C] Butt joint

D] Lap joint

Q 2] Combustion of oxy-acetylene flame produces about ________ degree

centigrade temperature]

A] 2400 to 2700

B] 1800 to 2200

C] 3100 to 3300

D] 1825 to 1875

Q 3] Acetylene gas is composed of carbon and ____________

A] argon

B] nitrogen

C] oxygen

D] Hydrogen

Q 4] The color of the acetylene gas cylinder is ______

A] green

B] black

C] maroon

D] Blue

Q 5] Which gas cylinder is also called as DA gas cylinder?

A] Acetylene gas cylinder

B] Oxygen gas cylinder

C] Argon gas cylinder

D] None of these

Q 6] 1 volume of liquid acetone can dissolve _______ volume of acetylene

gas under normal atmospheric pressure and temperature]

A] 10

B] 20

C] 25

D] 30

Q 7] Which one of the following is a type of gas regulator used in oxyacetylene

gas welding?

A] Single stage regulator

B] Double stage regulator

C] Both single and double stage regulator

D] None of these

Q 8] Identify the equipment shown in the picture]

A] Gas regulator

B] Welding blowpipe

C] Tip cleaner

D] Spark lighter

Q 9] In oxy acetylene gas cutting torch,the angle of the cutting nozzle with the body is ___ degree]

A] 45

B] 60

C] 90

D] 120

Q 10] In oxy acetylene gas welding blowpipe, the angle of the welding nozzle with the neck is ___ degree]

A] 45

B] 60

C] 90

D] 120

Q 11] How many control valves a welding blowpipe has, to control the flame?

A] 1
B] 2
C] 3
D] 4

Q 12] Leftward welding technique is also called as ______]
A] forward technique
B] backward technique
C] backhand technique
D] interior technique

Q 13] One function of flux in gas welding is ________]
A] to merge metal oxide
B] to reduce the melting point of the metal
C] to increase the temperature of flame
D] to clean hose pipe

Q 14] The liquid temperature of the filler metal used in brazing is more than________ degree centigrade]
A] 150
B] 450
C] 723
D] 100

Q 15] The size of cutting nozzle used in oxy- acetylene cutting process depends mainly on _____]
A] thickness of metal to be cut
B] purity of oxygen
C] duration of cut
D] type of cutting blowpipe

Q 16] Which of the following is a gas welding defect?
A] Crack
B] Porosity
C] Lack of fusion
D] All of these

Q 17] Which of the following is used to enlight the flame in oxy-acetylene gas cutting?
A] Electrode holder
B] Electrode
C] Spark lighter
D] Tip cleaner

Q 18] What is the unit of electric current?

B] Ampere

C] Ohm

D] Meter

Q 19] The pressure which makes the electric current to flow is called ________]

A] Electric current

B] Electric resistance

C] Conductivity

D] Voltage

Q 20] Which machine changes AC supply to DC in arc welding?

A] Transformer

B] Blow pipe

C] Welding rectifier

D] None of these

Q 21] Which of the following is AC welding machine?

A] DC motor generator

B] AC welding transformer

C] Rectifier set

D] None of these

Q 22] Which of the following is a welding position?

A] Flat

B] 2F

C] 3G

D] All of these

Q 24] Which of the following is an effect of long arc?

A] Less spatter

B] More fusion

C] More spatter

D] None of these

Q 25] An imaginary line passing through the weld center lengthwise is known as__________]

A] Weld rotation

B] Weld bead

C] Weld slop

D] Axis of weld

Q 26] Straight polarity is also called as_______]

A] DCEP

B] DCEN

C] MMAW

D] GMAW

Q 27] When the arc deviates from its regular path due to the magnetic disturbances it is called_______]

A] arc blow

B] overlap

C] undercut

D] arc trap

Q 28] Tip orifice of blowpipe nozzle should be cleaned with _____]

A] soft copper wire

B] steel wire

C] a small drill

D] tip cleaner

Q 29] Which of the following safety instruments is used to protect the eyes while doing grinding?

A] Hand screen

B] Helmet

C] Chipping goggles

D] Chipping screen

Q 30] Value of flux coating factor for light coated electrode is__________

A] 1]25 to 1]3

B] 1]4 to 1]5

C] 1]8 to 2]2

D] more than 2]2

Q 31] Which of the following is a cause of undercut in welding?

A] Current too high

B] Current too low

C] Use of long arc

D] None of these

Q 32] The third digit of number 7018 in American electrode coding E7018

indicates ______________]

A] Tensile strength of the joint

B] Welding position

C] Type of flux coating

D] Welding current and voltage condition

Q 33] Which type of power source is used in gas metal arc welding?

A] Constant voltage
B] Constant current
C] Constant resistance
D] None of these
Q 34] Which of the following metal transfer mode in MIG welding is also called as dip transfer?
A] Spray transfer
B] Short circuit transfer
C] Globular transfer
D] None of these
Q 35] Which of the following is a part of wire feeder of GMA welding?
A] Drive moter
B] Drive roller
C] Wire spool holder
D] All of these
Q 36] The last digit in American coding of GMAW wire electrode E 70S-2
indicates _____]
A] Tensile strength of the joint
B] chemical composition of wire
C] Type of flux coating
D] Welding current and voltage condition
Q 37] In FCAW, the deposition efficiency is generally in between________]
A] 20% to 30%
B] 30% to 45%
C] 60% to 66%
D] 80% to 86%
Q 38] Which of the following gas is used for shielding purpose in GMAW apart from argon?
A] carbon dioxide
B] nitrogen
C] oxygen
D] Hydrogen
Q 39] Which type of power source is used in TIG welding?
A] Constant voltage
B] Constant current
C] Constant resistance

D] None of these

Q 40] Which part of the TIG welding torch holds the electrode?

A] Nozzle

B] Collet

C] Back cap

D] Lead

Q 41] Gas nozzle of torch used in gas tungsten arc welding is made of ______]

A] plastic

B] copper

C] glass

D] Ceramic

Q 42] Identify the equipment shown in the picture]

A] Gas regulator

B] Flowmeter

C] Collet

D] Torch

Q 43] Melting point of pure tungsten is approximately ______ degrees centigrade]

A] 2050

B] 2550

C] 2830

D] 3380

Q 44] Which of the following statement is true?

A] Argon is a colourless gas

B] Argon is heavier than helium

C] Helium is a colourless gas

D] All of these

Q 45] What is the purpose of inert gas used in TIG welding?

A] To protect the molten metal from the atmospheric contamination

B] To contaminate in the weld metal

C] To stabilize the Arc

D] To get more spatters

Q 46] Which of the following statement is not true about submerged arc welding?

A] No spattering occur in this welding]

B] Welding can be done in flat position]

C] Welding can be done in overhead position]

D] None of these

Q 47] The electrode used in the spot welding is made up of which metal?

A] Copper

B] Brass

C] Carbon

D] Aluminium

Q 48] Which of the following can be easily be welded from flash butt welding process?

A] Cast iron

B] Lead

C] Brass

D] Mild steel

Q 49] Projection welding and seam welding are the types of ________ welding]

A] Gas metal arc welding

B] TIG welding

C] Resistance welding

D] Friction welding

Q 50] Which of the following should be used to remove slag and oxide after welding cast iron?

A] Tip cleaner

B] Ball peen hammer

C] Wire brush

D] None of these

Q 51] What type of filler rod should be selected to prevent weld decay in stainless steel welding?

A] Columbium base

B] Copper coated mild steel

C] Super silicon

D] None of these

Q 52] The preheating temperature of the workpiece can be checked by ________]

A] touching with finger

B] pyrometer

C] temperature indicating crayons

D] Thermocouple

Q 53] Which type of oxy-acetylene gas flame is used for gas welding of pure aluminium ?

A] Neutral

B] Carburising

C] Oxidising

D] None of these

Q 54] Which of the following is not a property of aluminium?

A] Good thermal conductivity

B] Good electrical conductivity

C] Light weight

D] Bad electrical conductivity

Q 55] Which of the following term is related to welding?

A] WPS

B] AWS

C] WPQ

D] All of these

Q 56] Izod and Charpy machines are related to ________ testing]

A] Impact

B] Ductility

C] Hardness

D] Creep

Q 57] Which quality of material can be tested with the help of Rockwell and Brinell test?

A] Hardness

B] Malleability

C] Elasticity

D] Ductility

Q 58] In dye penetrant test the penetrant passes into cracks by________ Action]

A] capillary

B] friction

C] radiation

D] Conduction

Q 59] In which of the following test, sound waves of high frequency are used?

A] Pressure test

B] Impact test

C] Radiography test

D] Ultrasonic test

Q 60] Gamma rays are produced by__________]

A] Iridium

B] Cobalt 60

C] Titanium

D] Tungste

Q 61] Which metal alloy is used to make contact tip of MIG welding torch?

\ MIG

A] Copper

B] Aluminium

C] Mild steel

D] Zinc

Q 62] Which shielding gas is used in TIG welding?

A] Hydrogen

B] Nitrogen

C] Argon

D] Ozone

Q 63] Which of these is not a resistance welding process?

A] Projection welding

B] Seam welding

C] Flash butt welding

D] Carbon arc welding

Q 64] A single V edge preparation is used when plates .... thick are to be welded]

A] 1 to 5 mm

B] 5 to 15 mm

C] 15 to 25 mm

D] More than 25 mm

Q 65] The welding process which requires flux in granular form is ....

A] Gas welding

B] Submerged arc welding

C] Manual metal arc welding

D] Thermit welding

Q 66] The oxy-acetylene flame used for welding of aluminium is

A] Oxidizing flame

B] Neutral flame

C] Neutral flame with little haze of excess oxygen

D] Neutral flame with little haze of excess acetylene

Q 67] A device used to keep the parts to be welded in alignment is called]]]]]

A] Welding jig

B] Welding fixture

C] Welding positioner

D] Welding manipulator

Q 68] The process which uses non-consumable electrode is ....

A] TIG

B] MIG

C] MAG

D] SAW

Q 69] What will happen if the blowpipe while gas cutting is moved to and fro frequently?

A] The kerf will be narrow

B] The kerf will be wide

C] There will be no effect on the kerf

D] The kerf will be of correct size

Q 70] Cast iron can be best welded by ....

A] MIG welding

B] TIG welding

C] Arc welding

D] Gas welding

Q 71] What type of weld is obtained when two pieces of flat bar are joined to form T ?

A] Butt

B] Fillet

C] Lap

D] Edge

Q 72] Which type of non-destructive test is suitable to check the internal defects in high pressure boiler welding?

A] Radiographic test

B] Visual test

C] Magnetic particle test

D] Dye penetrant test

forge welding

Q 73] Which of these is an example of plastic welding?

A] Arc welding

B] Gas welding

C] Thermit welding

D] Forge welding

Q 74] Which of these rays are not produced during arc welding?

A] Infrared rays

B] Ultraviolet rays

C] Visible light rays

D] Gamma rays

Q 75] Heat-affected-zone is that portion of the metal which ....

A] Melts and becomes plastic

B] Neither melts nor becomes plastic

C] Melts but does not become plastic

D] Doesn't melt but becomes plastic

Q 76] AWS code for electrodes starts with E followed by a 4 digit number]

The third digit represents ....

A] Type of flux coating

B] Welding position

C] Tensile strength of weldment

D] Polarity

Q 77] One of the reasosn to avoid the use of long arc during welding is that ....

A] It increases open circuit voltage

B] It gives lack of fusion of base metal

C] The joint will develop cracks during welding

D] It consumes more electrodes

Q 78] During magnetic particle testing , the best practice is to]

A] Use AC whenever possible

B] Use DC whenever possible

C] Use at least 100 amperes

D] Magnetize the part in two directions at right angle to each other

Q 79] A circle used in the welding symbol means that welding is

A] To be all around the joint

B] To ensure that the subsequent deposits are sound

C] To relieve stresses in the first place

D] To remove any excess slag

Q 80] In a welded joint, the minimum distance from the root to the weld face is]]]]]]]]]

A] Leg

B] Effective throat

C] Length of the weld

D] Depth of the weld

Q 81] Which of these is the basic characteristic of submerged arc welding?

A] Deep penetration

B] Smooth weld

C] High welding current

D] All of these

Q 82] Among the four modes of metal transfer in GMAW, which one is least desirable?

A] Spray

B] Short-circuiting

C] Globular

D] Pulsed-spray

Q 83] For gas metal arc welding of mild steel, the suitable shielding gas is]]]]]]]]]

A] Carbon dioxide

B] Argon

C] Helium

D] Mixture of argon and helium

Q 84] What will happen in TIG welding if tungsten electrode is connected

to positive terminal?

A] It will cause porosity in the weld bead

B] Weld penetration will be shallow and wide

C] There will be cracks in weld bead

D] There will be lack of fusion

Q 85] What should be the shape of electrode tip for TIG welding of mild steel?

B] Spherical end

C] Pointed end

D] Angular end

residual stresses

Q 86] What should be done to reduce residual stresses caused due to welding?

A] Allow the parts to move freely during welding

B] Use "back step" sequence

C] Use post weld heat treatment

D] Use "back step" sequence and / or post weld heat treatment

Q 87] The problem of arc blow is likely to happen when ....

A] Welding with direct current

B] Welding with alternating current

C] Welding with bare electrodes

D] Welding with alternating current and / or bare electrodes

Q 88] It is preferred to have welding shield in black colour] Why?

A] It gives good appearance

B] It better reflects light rays

C] It absorbs light rays

D] It reduces cost of shield

Q 89] Which property of metals helps in retaining the molten metal deposited on the joint when welding in overhead position?

A] Density

B] Magnetic attraction

C] Thermal contraction

D] Surface tension

Q 90] What defect is likely to be caused if too high welding current is used?

A] Undercut

B] Porosity

C] Lack of fusion

D] Excessive penetration

Q 91] What defect will happen to the joint if large weld puddle is deposited in MIG-MAG welding?

A] Undercut

B] Lack of fusion

C] Cracks

D] Lack of penetration

Q 92] Which of these is one of the advantages of using iron powder electrodes?

A] It avoids cracks in the joint

B] It reduces time required to complete the weld

C] It increases the strength of the flux coating

D] It improves flow of current through the electrode

Q 93] The filler wire used in MIG / MAG welding is copper coated] Why?

A] To prevent base metal reaction

B] To prevent rust

C] To prevent contamination by air

D] To prevent gas shield

Q 94] Different shielding gases are used in MIG / MAG welding] Which gas

produces more stable arc than others?

A] Argon

B] Helium

C] Carbon dioxide

D] Hydrogen

Q 95] Guided bend test is used to determine ....

A] Ductility

B] Tensile strength

C] Impact value

D] Percentage elongation

Q 96] If cylinder trolley is not available, how should a gas cylinder be moved?

A] Dragging

B] Sliding

C] Rolling

D] Tilting and moving

Q 97] While gas cutting , the nozzle should be..........

A] Touching the work

B] 2 mm from the work

C] 5 mm from the work

D] 10 mm from the work

Q 98] What is the process called that removes metal from the surface of a plate to a desired depth?

A] Beveling

B] Grooving

C] Gouging

D] Piercing

Q 99] If the fusion of the bead with the base metal is poor, what could be the probable cause?

A] Current is too high

B] Current is too low

C] Arc is too short

D] Electrode travel is too slow

Q 100] When depositing the root run on an open corner joint in vertical position, it is necessary to maintain short arc and a key hole] Why?

A] To avoid distortion

B] To avoid arc getting unstable

C] To obtain good penetration

D] To facilitate for the welder to weld

Q 101] What makes it difficult to weld cast iron?

A] Its hardness and brittleness

B] Its high compressive strength

C] Its low melting point

D] Its fluidity

Q 102] One of the advantages of using DC welding machine for welding is..........

A] Low maintenance cost

B] Low welding cost

C] Low power consumption

D] Both ferrous and non-ferrous metals can be welded

Q 103] The percentage of carbon by weight in acetylene gas is

A] 92]3%

B] 89]3%

C] 85]3%

D] 78]3%

Q 104] What is the system called when three or more gas cylinders are connected together?

A] Group system

B] Compound system

C] Series system

D] Manifold system

Q 105] What type of fire extinguisher is suitable for use in welding shop?

A] Foam type of extinguisher

B] Dry powder extinguisher

C] Carbon dioxide extinguisher

D] Halon extinguisher

Q 106] Which type of pipes are welded by uphill welding technique?

A] Thin wall pipes

B] Thick wall pipes

C] Big diameter pipes

D] Small diameter pipes

Q 107] A casting having a crack is to be repaired by welding] How will you

prevent extension of the crack while welding?

A] BY preheating

B] By grooving the crack

C] By tacking at both ends of the crack

D] By drilling at both ends of the crack

Q 108] Which resistance welding process will be used for welding thin sheets continuously?

A] Spot welding

B] Seam welding

C] Projection welding

D] Flash welding

Q 109] Which one of the following pipe welding positions represents 45°

inclined position welding?

A] 1 - G

B] 2 - G

C] 5 - G

D] 6 – G

Q 110] What will happen if long arc is used in MMAW?

A] The joint will be strong

B] There will be lack of fusion of base metal

C] The joint will develop cracks

D] The consumption of electrodes will be high

Q 111] Which metal does not allow X - rays to pass through it?

A] Copper

B] Zinc

C] Tin

D] Lead

Q 112] Which type of welding requires the use of electrode in the form of

spool?

A] Stick welding

B] MIG welding

C] Oxy-acetylene welding

D] Manual metal arc welding

Q 113] Argon is used for welding of stainless steel because..........

A] It is inert

B] It helps in melting of the electrode

C] It is cheap

D] It prevents porosity

Q 114] The term "square wave" is related to..........

A] Shape of output power

B] Shape of tungsten electrode

C] Shape of power source control box

D] Shape of filler metal

Q 115] Which property of metal has the biggest influence on distortion during welding?
A] Modulus of elasticity
B] Coefficient of thermal expansion
C] Coefficient of thermal conductivity
D] Yield strength
Q 116] How to avoid blowholes in weld bead during MIG welding?
A] By increasing the speed of welding
B] By increasing stick-out
C] By setting high current
D] By concentrating shielding gas on weld bead
Q 117] Helium is lighter than argon by ....
A] Six times
B] Eight times
C] Ten times
D] Fifteen times
Q 118] If the plates to be welded are clamped, how will it affect warping?
A] It will have no effect on warping
B] It will decrease warping
C] It will increase warping
D] It will have negligible effect on warping
Q 119] Which one of the following is most likely to cause burn through welding?
A] Root face too small
B] Travel speed too fast
C] Root gap too small
D] Travel speed too slow
Q 120] What is the advantage of using copper instead of aluminium in welding cables?
A] Copper is cheaper
B] Copper is lighter
C] Copper improves current carrying capacity and flexibility
D] All of these
Q 121] A triangular-shaped weld symbol represents what type of weld?
A] Fillet weld
B] Bevel groove
C] Flare groove
D] V groove

Q 1) In resistance welding

1) No arc is produced

2) Heat is produced by passage of current

3) No filler metal is used

4) All of these/येसभी

Q 2) Which of these is NOT a type of distortion taking place in welding?

1) Radial distortion

2) Longitudinal distortion

3) Angular distortion

4) Transverse distortion/

Q 3) Identify the defect in the weld bead shown below.

1) Blowhole

2) Lack of fusion

3) Lack of penetration

4) Porosity

Q 4) The function of welding torch in TIG welding is

1) To carry current to weld area

2) To carry shielding gas to weld area

3) To carry cooling water

4) All of these

Q 5) A short weld made prior to welding to hold plates in alignment is called

1) Tack weld

2) Stitch weld

3) Tag weld

4) Temporary weld

Q 6) Determining the quality of weld without destroying the weld, is a method called

1) TDT

2) NDT

3) PDT

4) QDT

Q 7) Which of these is a method of Welding with pressure ?

1) Gas welding

2) Resistance welding

3) Manual Metal Arc Welding

4) Thermit (Fusion) welding

Q 8) Which of these is a temporary joint?

1) Press fit joint
2) Welded joint
3) Brazed joint
4) Riveted joint

Q 9) Which of these is NOT a component of arc welding circuit?
1) Power source
2) Welding cable
3) Jig
4) Electrode holder with electrode

Q 10) As the length of the welding arc increases
1) The operating voltage increases
2) The operating voltage decreases
3) The operating voltage remains the same
4) The operating voltage may increase or decrease

Q 11) Which of these is used to check shape and size of a weld bead?
1) Weld indicator
2) Weld template
3) Weld gauge
4) Weld dial

Q 12) Which of these machines converts AC into DC?
1) Amplifier
2) Inverter
3) Rectifier
4) Transformer

Q 13) The problem of arc blow is encountered when
1) Tranformer is used for welding
2) DC power supply is used for welding
3) When rectifier is used for welding
4) Any of the above is used

Q 14) In the figure of gas cutting torch shown below, which component controls flow of cutting oxygen?
1) Flow of cutting oxygen is controlled by A
2) Flow of cutting oxygen is controlled by B
3) Flow of cutting oxygen is controlled by C
4) Flow of cutting oxygen is controlled by D

Q 15) Electrical potential is also known by the name/ विद्युत ?मता को ________ नाम से

1) Electrical force

2) Electromotive force

3) Electrolytic force

4) Electromagnetic force

Q 16) Name the resistance welding process in which two wheels are used.

1) Silent butt welding

2) Flash butt welding

3) Seam welding

4) Projection welding

Q 17) In spot welding, electrodes are made of

2) Copper

3) Tungsten

4) Tin

Q 18) Which of these metals can be welded by TIG welding?

1) Copper

2) Aluminium

3) Stainless steel

4) All of these

Q 19) Which shielding gas is preferred for TIG welding of copper?

1) Argon

2) Helium

3) Mixture of argon and helium

4) Both argon and helium are equally good

Q 20) For TIG welding of aluminium, use of

1) DC with electrode positive gives better results

2) DC with electrode negative gives better results

3) AC gives better results

4) Any one of above will give good results

gas welding

Q 21) Which of these is NOT a high speed welding process?

1) Submerged arc welding

2) MIG welding

3) MAG welding

4) Gas welding

Q 22) What is NOT true about MIG welding process?

1) No slag is formed

2) No frequent change of electrode is required

3) Equipment required is expensive

4) Rate of metal deposition is slow

Q 23) Figure below shows gas cutting process. Kerf is indicated by

1) Kerf is indicated by A

2) Kerf is indicated by B

3) Kerf is indicated by C

4) Kerf is indicated by D

Q 24) Identify type of metal transfer in MIG welding as shown below

1) Dip transfer

2) Spray transfer

3) Globular transfer

4) None of these

Q 25) What is chemical formula of calcium carbide?

1) CaC

2) CaC2

3) Ca2C

4) Ca2C2

Q 26) Which of these is reducing agent or deoxidant?

1) Silicon

2) Manganese

3) Both of the above

4) None of these

Q 27) If a metal resists penetration, it is

1) Tough

2) Brittle

3) Hard

4) Ductile

Q 28) Figure below is simplified diagram of a transformer.

1) In it B indicated iron core

2) In it B indicates copper core
3) In it B indicates steel core
4) In it B indicates regulating core

Q 29) Why is cast iron preheated before welding?
1) To avoid shrinkage
2) To avoid cracking
3) To avoid hardening
4) To ensure all of the above

Q 30) In arc welding, closed butt joint is used on plated upto
1) 3 mm thick
2) 5 mm thick
3) 8 mm thick
4) 10 mm thick

Q 31) The test which does not require use of electricity is
1) X - ray testing
2) Dye penetrant testing
3) Ultasonic testing
4) Hydraulic pressure testing

Q 32) What is arc time ?
1) The time the arc is on during the arc welding operation
2) The total time the worker is clocked into work
3) The non – arc time
4) The total arc and non – arc time

Q 33) Identify the joint shown below
1) Edge joint
2) Corner joint
3) Plug joint
4) Slot joint

Q 34) What is NOT correct about flux used in gas welding?
1) It is fusible
2) It is chemical compound
3) It dissolves oxides
4) None of these

Q 35) When gas welding, flux is not required for ......
1) Aluminium
2) Mild steel
3) Copper
4) Brass

Q 36) Visual examination of weld can help detect the defect

1) Undercut

2) Improper profile

3) Incomplete penetration

4) All of these

Q 37) What is the type of pipe joint shown in figure below?

1) Tee joint

2) Flange joint

3) Y joint

4) Branch joint

Q 38) The size of the cutting nozzle used in oxy-acetylene cutting depends mainly on

1) Thickness of the metal to be cut

2) Purity of oxygen

3) Duration of cut

4) Type of the cutting blowpipe

Q 39) How should the orifice of a blowpipe be cleaned?

1) Use soft steel wire

2) Use soft copper wire

3) Use tip cleaner

4) Use a small diameter drill

Q 40) The major part of atmospheric air is taken by

1) Oxygen

2) Nitrogen

3) Hydrogen

4) Argon

Q 41) The letter H used as a suffix at the end of the electrode code indicates that it is ....

1) Heavy coated electrode

2) Low hydrogen electrode

3) Iron powder electrode

4) High tensile strength electrode

Q 42) Which test is done to find out percentage elongation of weldment?

1) Guided bend test

2) Tensile test

3) Fatigue test

4) Impact test

Q 43) Which welding defect can be easily detected by visual examination?

1) Lack of fusion

2) Misalignment of welded parts

3) Inter-bead slag inclusion

4) Root defect in T - fillet weld

Q 44) What will be the effect of long electrode stick-out in MIG / MAG welding

1) Excess weld metal

2) Low weld metal

3) Weld metal rough

4) Weld metal smooth

Q 45) Which inert gas will produce more stable arc in GMAW?

1) Argon

2) Helium

3) Carbon dioxide

4) All of these produce equally stable arc

Q 46) Which operating variable in submerged arc welding controls the arc length?

1) Welding speed

2) Welding voltage

3) Welding current

4) Electrode wire extension

Q 47) What is the size of gas nozzle for 1.5 mm diameter tungsten electrode in TIG welding

process?

1) 10 mm diameter

2) 12 mm diameter

3) 14 mm diameter

4) 16 mm diameter

Q 48) Identify the weld defect in the bead shown in figure below.

1) Porosity

2) Slag inclusion

3) Lack of fusion

4) Lack of penetration

Q 49) One of the reasons for avoiding use of long arc in welding is ....

1) It gives lack of fusion in base metal

2) It increases open circuit voltage

3) It increases proability of crack in weld

4) It increases consumption of electrodes

Q 50) Application of which NDT does not require electricity?

1) X - ray test

2) Dye penetrant test

3) Ultrasonic test

4) Hydraulic pressure test

Q 51) The principal advantage because of which iron powder electrodes are used, is ....

1) Time required to complete the weld is reduced

2) There will be no cracks in the weld

3) Flux coating becomes stronger

4) Resistance to flow of current is reduced

Q 52) Which statement is true about submerged arc welding?

1) vacuum Welding is done

2) Bare wire electrode is used

3) It can be applied for welding in any position

4) Rate of metal deposition is slow

Q 53) What is the advantage of using low heat input electrodes?

1) Very thin layer of weld metal can be applied

2) Distortion and warpage are reduced

3) Quality of weld metal is high

4) Surfacing can be done in all positions

Q 54) The welding symbol shown below is of ....

1) Square butt weld

2) Single - V butt weld

3) Double - V butt weld

4) Single - U butt weld

Q 55) What will be the effect of improper inert gas flow in TIG welding?

1) Porosity

2) Cracks

3) Lack of penetration

4) Weld metal getting oxidised

Q 56) Which electronic unit facilitates arc initiation in TIG welding?

1) Low frequency unit

2) Medium frequency unit

3) High frequency unit

4) Double frequency unit

Q 57) The nozzle used in TIG welding is made of ....

1) Bakelite

2) Ceramic

3) Plastic

4) Clay

Q 58) What will be defect if fusion does not take place up to root of the weld?

1) Blowholes

2) Lack of penetration

3) Porosity

4) Cracks

Q 59) Which non-destructive test can determine the depth of an internal weld defect?

1) Ultrasonic test

2) Magnetic particle test

3) Dye penetrant test

4) Eddy current test

Q 60) Which physical property helps to retain molten metal in position when welding is

being done in overhead position?

1) Magnetic attraction

2) Surface tension

3) Capillarity

4) Thermal contraction

Q 61) What is the shape of the tip of tungsten electrode used for TIG welding of

aluminium?

1) Pointed end

2) Flat end

3) Spherical end

4) Angular end

Q 62) Spot welding process basically depends upon ....

1) Application of forging pressure

2) Ohmic resistance

3) Generation of heat

4) Generation of heat and application of forging pressure

Q 63) There are four modes of metal transfer in GMAW. Which one is considered least desirable?

1) Spray

2) Pulsed spray

3) Globular

4) Short circuiting

Q 64) What type of electrodes are used in resistance seam welding?

1) Flat

2) Disc

3) Domed

4) Pointed

Q 65) Flux is required to be used in .... process.

1) TIG

2) MIG

3) MAG

4) SAW

Q 66) What is the preheat temperature to weld carbon steel pieces having 0.3% to 0.45% carbon?

1) 100 to120 C

2) 150 to 280 C

3) 280 to 350 C

4) 350 to 450 C

Q 67) Carbon supplied by the carburizing flame in gas welding makes the weld metal

....

1) Tough

2) Ductile

3) Brittle

4) Hard and brittle

Q 68) It is difficult to weld copper by resistance welding because of its ...

1) High thermal conductivity

2) High electrical conductivity

3) High toughness

4) High ductility

Q 69) What will happen if cast iron is welded without preheating?

1) Porosity

2) Undercut

3) Crack

4) Blowholes

Q 70) Which resistance welding machine is used to join pipe sections end-to-end?

1) Spot welding machine
2) Projection welding machine
3) Butt welding machine
4) Seam welding machine

Q 71) What is the purpose of setting root gap (g in figure below) in a butt joint?

1) To obtain required depth of penetration
2) To control distortion
3) To maintain proper alignment
4) To deposit more metal

Q 72) Cast iron welding should be completed as quickly as possible. If slow welding is

done, it will cause burning of ....

1) Iron and phosphorus
2) Copper and iron
3) Carbon and silicon
4) Lead and phosphorus

Q 73) The type of joint used in spot welding is ....

1) Butt welding
2) Lap welding
3) Corner welding
4) Edge welding

Q 74) If three or more gas cylinders are connected together, the system is called ....

1) Portable system
2) Group system
3) Manifold system
4) High pressure system

Q 75) What may happen if a welder is arc welding while standing on wet floor?

1) Burn injury
2) Electric shock
3) Cut on the leg
4) Eye injury

Q 76) Which main factor will help cost of welding in a single V butt joint?

1) Weaving technique used
2) Correct included angle of V
3) Length of arc
4) Type of welding current used

Q 77) The zone next of the fusion zone in a welded joint is called ..
2) Adjacent zone
3) Heat-affected zone
4) Local zone

Q 78) Which of these metals has the highest thermal conductivity?
1) Mild steel
2) Copper
3) Aluminium
4) Zinc

Q 79) Oxy-acetylene cutting torch tip orifice should be cleaned with ....
1) Tip cleaner
2) Copper wire
3) Steel wire
4) Small size drill

Q 80) One of the reasons for avoiding the use of long arc in arc welding is ....
1) It will increase open circuit voltage
2) It will give lack of fusion of base metal
3) The joint will develop cracks
4) It will increase consumptionof electrodes

Q 81) What will be the effect on distortion if the number of passes to complete a joint is
increased?
1) It will increase distortion
2) It will decrease distortion
3) It will have no effect on distortion
4) It will have very little effect on distortion

Q 82) Root bend test is used to test the amount of weld ....
1) Ductility
2) Elongation
3) Hardness
4) Penetration

Q 83) When water reacts with calcium carbide, the gas produced is ....

1) Hydrogen
2) Acetylene
3) Argon
4) Methane

Q 84) The circle used in a welding symbol means that welding is ....
1) To ensure that subsequent deposits are sound
2) To be all around the joint
3) To remove any excess flux
4) To relieve stresses in the first place

Q 85) In the iG position of pipe welding, the pipe must be ....
1) Rotated
2) Inclined
3) Horizontal
4) Vertical

Q 86) Which of these is a non-destructive test?
1) Nick break test
2) Impact test
3) Tensile test
4) Magnetic particle test

Q 87) The portion of the base metal that has not melted during welding but its

microstructure has changed, is called _______
1) Fusion zone
2) Heat-affected zone
3) Dead zone
4) Twilight zone

Q 88) The heating of a welded joint immediately after having completed, it is called ..
1) Post heating
2) Delayed heating
3) Late heating
4) Fast heating

Q 89) Which of these welding processes requires the use of granular flux?
1) TIG welding
2) MIG welding
3) Submerged arc welding
4) Manual Metal Arc Welding

Q 90) What will happen if during TIG welding, tungsten electrode melts and deposits on

weld metal?

1) Cracks will develop

2) There will be poor penetration

3) Weld metal will get contaminated

4) There will be lack of fusion

Q 91) What can cause excessive burning of electrodes in arc welding?

1) Arc blow

2) Long arc length

3) Low quality electrodes

4) Too high welding current

Q 92) Which non-destructive test does not require supply from any power source?

1) X - ray test

2) Ultrasonic test

3) Dye penetrant test

4) Hydraulic pressure test

Q 93) What can happen if you see electric arc with naked eye?

1) Electric shock

2) Eye injury

3) Burn injury

4) Cut on legs and hands

Q 94) Which of these is one of the factors included in classification and coding of

electrodes?

1) Type of flux coating

2) Length of electrode

3) Core diameter of electrode

4) Required baking temperature of electrode

Q 95) The property of a metal which enables it to stretch, bend or twist without cracking is called ....

1) Ductility

2) Malleability

3) Hardness

4) Toughness

Q 96) Which method of weld inspection is the cheapest?

1) Radiography

2) Ultrasonic test

3) Magnetic particle test

4) Visual examination

Q 97) What is the type of filler wire used in submerged arc welding?

1) Bare wire

2) Lightly coated wire

3) Heavily coated wired

4) Flux cored wire

Q 98) Which of these is an example of plastic welding?

1) Arc welding

2) Gas welding

3) Forge welding

4) Thermit welding

Q 99) Double V or double U edge preparation is normally used if the thickness of plates to

be welded is ....

1) 1 - 5 mm

2) 5 - 10 mm

3) 10 - 15 mm

4) More than 15 mm

Q 100) The tip of a gas welding blowpipe is made of ....

1) Brass

2) Bronze

3) Copper

4) Mild steel

Q 101) Which of these is a temporary joint?

1) Welded joint

2) Press fit joint

3) Brazed joint

4) Riveted joint

Q 102) What is the storage medium used to store acetylene gas in a cylinder at high

pressure?

1) Petroleum jelly

2) Kerosene oil

3) Acetone

4) Water

Q 103) As a matter of safety never use .... on gas cylinders and regulators.

1) Wrench

2) Oil

3) Teflone tape

4) Leak detector

Q 104) Which oxy-acetylene flame contains excess of fuel gas?

1) Oxidising flame

2) Carburizing flame

3) Neutral flame

4) Standard flame

Q 105) Which is the most common (maximum percentage) gas in the atmosphere?

1) Oxygen

2) Nitrogen

3) Carbon dioxide

4) Methane

Q 106) An electric circuit is a path taken by flow of current. A path with no breaks is called

....

1) Closed circuit

2) Open circuit

3) Limited circuit

4) Continuous circuit

Q 107) Heat is measured in the units called ....

1) Newton

2) Joule

3) Watt

4) Celsius

Q 108) Always use .... to light a gas welding torch.

1) Matches

2) Striker

3) Electric arc

4) Cigarette lighter

Q 109) What term relates to amount of current flowing in an electric circuit?

1) Volt

2) Ampere

3) Ohm

4) Hertz

Q 110) What should be used to clean the tip of gas welding torch?

1) Steel wire

2) Copper wire

3) Copper coated steel wire

4) Tip cleaner

Q 111) Which among the following has relatively the highest thermal conductivity?

1) Zinc

2) Mild steel

3) Copper

4) Aluminium

Q 112) In case of oxy-acetylene welding, oxygen cylinders are painted ....

1) White

2) Black

3) Maroon

4) Red

Q 113) Which gas welding flame is better suited to weld both ferrous and non-ferrous

metals?

1) Oxy-LPG flame

2) Oxy-acetylene flame

3) Oxy-hydrogen flame

4) Air-acetylene flame

Q 114) What is used to remove slag from a weld bead?

1) Mallet

2) Chipping hammer

3) Claw hammer

4) Sledge hammer

Q 1) The walls of welding shop should be painted

1) Dark colour

2) White colour

3) Reflecting colour

4) None of these

Q 2) For safety purpose, what is NOT good practice?

1) Use oil or grease on cylinder fittings

2) Keep cylinders cool

3) Not to use cylinders as rollers

4) Not to use cylinders as anvils

Q 3) What should be arc length in manual metal arc welding?

1) Approximately equal to electrode wire dia.

2) Approximately equal to half electrode wire dia.

3) Aproximately equal to double elecrode wire dia

4) Approximately equal to 1.5 times electrode wire dia.

Q 4) Which of these electrodes coating provides additional weld metal during welding?

1) Iron powder electrode

2) Mineral silicate

3) Calcium fluoride

4) Metal carbonate

Q 5) In dye penetrant test, the liquid dye is pulled out of the discontinuity by virtue of which

action?

1) Heating

2) Cooling

3) Suction

4) Capillary

Q 6) Before fixing regulator on gas cylinder, the valve is opened a quarter turn and then

closed immediately. What is this action called?

1) Checking

2) Setting

3) Testing

4) Cracking

Q 7) In figure given below, identify A and B .

1) A - Slopc; B - Rotation

2) A - Inclination; B - Rotation

3) A - Slope; B - Inversion

4) A - Angle; B – Turning

Q 8) A welded joint is fixed on a vice and bent by hammering. What is this test called?

1) Free bend tes

2) Nick break test

3) Fillet fracture test

4) None of these

Q 9) A welded joint is subjected to push and pull forces alternatively for a long time. What is this test called?

1) Impact test
2) Tensile test
3) Fatigue test
4) Hardness test

Q 10) In the welding circuit shown below, what does 2 represent?

1) Primary winding
2) Secondary winding
3) Current regulator
4) Rectifier

Q 11) Welding symbol consists of 7 elements. Which one is NOT among them?

1) Reference line
2) Arrow
3) Dimensions and other details
4) Auxiliary symbols

Q 12) Which metal gets easily oxidised even at room temperature?

1) Coppe
2) Aluminium
3) Chromium
4) All of these

Q 13) What welding process is shown in figure given below?

1) MIG welding
2) Submerged arc welding
3) MAG welding
4) Thermit welding

Q 14) What part of a file is hardened and tempered?

1) Handle
2) Tang
3) Ferrule
4) Body

Q 15) What could be the reason for a hacksaw bladee getting loose after a few strokes?

1) The blade is stretched
2) Wing nut is worn out
3) Pitch of the blade is wrong

4) Selection of set of saw is wrong

Q 16) What difficulty is likely to be faced in welding of medium carbon steel?

1) Weld metal becomes brittle

2) Weld metal becomes hard

3) It will crack if cooled rapidly

4) All of these

Q 17) What is the effect of carbon supplied by carburising oxy-acetylene flame?

1) It makes the weld tough

2) It makes the weld ductile

3) It makes the metal brittle

4) It makes the metal hard and brittle

Q 18) At the end of a weld bead, the electrode is moved backward for about 10 mm

gradually increasing the electrode angle from 70 degree to 90 degree. Why is this technique applied?

1) To reduce distortion

2) To avoid undercuts

3) To avoid crater

4) To avoid inclusion of slag

Q 19) Which method is suitable to avoid angular distortion (figure below) in a single V butt joint by arc welding?

1) By using skip welding

2) By locating parts out-of-position

3) By intermittent welding

4) By keeping divergence allownance

Q 20) While brazing the job got overheated. How will you manipulate the torch to overcome the problem that may be caused due to overheating?

1) Increase the gap between the flame cone and the job

2) Increase the torch angle

3) Reduce the speed of welding

4) Increase the speed of welding

Q 21) While it is easy to cut mild steel plates by oxy-acetylene flame, it is NOT so with

aluminium plates. Why?

1) There is no change in colour of aluminium when it is heated

2) The melting point of aluminium oxide is high

3) The melting point of aluminium is low

4) Thermal expansion of aluminium is high

Q 22) A cracked cast iron piece is to be repaired by gas welding. How will you control the extension of the crack during welding?

1) By preheating

2) By grooving the crack

3) By tacking at both ends of the crack

4) By drilling at both ends of the crack

Q 23) What safe storage medium is used to store acetylene in the cylinder at high pressure?

1) Water

2) Acetone

3) Kerosene

4) Petroleum jelly

Q 24) It is best to use a trolley when a gas cylinder is to be moved from one place to another in the workshop. If trolley is NOT available, how should a cylinder be moved?

1) By dragging

2) By rolling

3) By sliding

4) By tilting at an angle and moving

Q 25) What will be the effect on the joint, if the gap between the plates to be brazed is

more?

1) Less distortion

2) Less capillary action

3) More joint strength

4) Better joint appearance

Q 26) What is the pipe welding position as shown in figure given below?

1) 1G

2) 2G

3) 5G

4) 6G

Q 27) Figure given below relates to oxy-acetylene cutting. It is mentioned Maintain correct distance. How much should it be?

1) 1 mm

2) 5 mm

3) 10 mm

4) 20 mm

Q 28) What is the technique of gas welding as shown in figure below?

1) Left-ward welding

2) Right-ward welding

3) Side-ward welding

4) Normal welding

Q 29) What should be the shade number of filter glass to be used for arc welding with 150 ampere current?

1) Shade numer 6

2) Shade number 8

3) Shade number....... 10

4) Shade number 22

Q 30) The open circuit voltage normally ranges between .... in case of welding

transformers.

1) 50 - 70 V

2) 70 - 90 V

3) 90 - 110 V

4) 110 - 130 V

Q 31) The open circuit voltage normally ranges between .... in case of welding

rectifiers.

1) 30 - 60 V

2) 50 - 80 V

3) 80 - 110 V

4) 110 - 140 V

Q 32) Before a regulator is fixed on gas cylinder, the valve is opened momentarily and then closed immediately. The purpose is to clear the dirt. What is this action called?

1) Checking

2) Clearing

3) Cracking

4) Cleaning

Q 33) Which defect in T - fillet weld can be detected by nick break test?

1) Crater cracks

2) Surface cracks

3) Lack of root penetration

4) Insufficient throat thickness

Q 34) As per Indian Standards, electrode coding contains two letters followed by a 4-digit number. What detail is given by the fourth digit?

1) Tensile strength
2) Welding position
3) Percentage elongation
4) Welding current and voltage condition

Q 35) Oxy-acetylene cutting torch can be used to cut easily ....

1) Stainless steel
2) Cast iron
3) Carbon steel
4) Aluminium

Q 36) In arc welding, the problem of arc blow can be avoided by ....

1) Using AC welding machine
2) Using bare electrodes
3) Increasing arc length
4) Welding away from earth connection

Q 37) In coding of electrodes, radiographic quality of electrodes is indicated by letter

1) A
2) X
3) Y
4) Z

Q 38) Which type of flux coated electrodes are used in fusion welding of cast iron?

1) Basic type
2) Rutile type
3) Cellulose type
4) Iron oxide type

Q 39) What is the function of earth clamp as used in arc welding?

1) Hold the electrode firmly during welding
2) Connect the electrode firmly during welding
3) Connect the earthing cable to workpiece
4) Conduct current from earthing cable to electrode

Q 40) The capacity of an arc welding machine is indicated by ....

1) Open circuit voltage
2) Closed circuit voltage
3) Input current in ampere
4) Output current in ampere

Q 41) Why is welding helmet made black in colour?
1) It gives pleasing appearance
2) It better reflects light
3) It absorbs light
4) It reduces its cost
Q 42) A ball pein hammer is specified by ....
1) Its weight
2) Length of its handle
3) Shape of its face
4) Material of its head

welding defects

Q 43) Before tack welding of pipes, a 1.5 mm bent wire is placed between the pipes. What is its purpose?
1) To prevent welding defects
2) To maintain uniform gap
3) To increase weld strength
4) To prevent distortion
Q 44) What is the effect of having long arc in arc welding?
1) Arc becomes unstable
2) Metal deposition is correct
3) Electrode burns evenly
4) There is no wastage in electrode burning
Q 45) Which welding machine has commutator as one of its parts?
1) Motor generator set
2) Welding transformer
3) Welding rectifier
4) Engine driven set

Q 46) This is the zone in a welded joint which has not melted but its microstructure has

changed.

1) Local zone

2) Base zone

3) Heat-affected zone

4) Cold zone

Q 47) The inclination of the torch to workpiece in rightward technique in gas welding

is...................

1) 30°–40°

2) 40°–50°

3) 50°–60°

4) 60°–70°

Q 48) What is the function of gas regulator provided on gas cylinder?

1) To obtain different types of flames

2) To mix gases in required proportion

3) To vary volume of gas supply

4) To set working pressure

Q 49) In which welding position the rate of filler metal deposition is more?

1) Flat position

2) Vertical position

3) Horizontal position

4) Overhead position

Q 1) In resistance welding

INDUSTRIAL TRAINING INSTITUTE

Monthly Test-1, Marks- 20, Date:- ______________

(Every Question Carry Two Marks)

1) No arc is produced

2) Heat is produced by passage of current

3) No filler metal is used

4) All of these/ये सभी

Q 2) Which of these is NOT a type of distortion taking place in welding?

1) Radial distortion

2) Longitudinal distortion

3) Angular distortion

4) Transverse distortion/

Q 3) Identify the defect in the weld bead shown below.

1) Blowhole

2) Lack of fusion

3) Lack of penetration

4) Porosity

Q 4) The function of welding torch in TIG welding is

1) To carry current to weld area

2) To carry shielding gas to weld area

3) To carry cooling water

4) All of these

Q 5) A short weld made prior to welding to hold plates in alignment is called

1) Tack weld

2) Stitch weld

3) Tag weld

4) Temporary weld

Q 6) Determining the quality of weld without destroying the weld, is a method called

1) TDT

2) NDT

3) PDT

4) QDT

Q 7) Which of these is a method of Welding with pressure ?

1) Gas welding

2) Resistance welding

3) Manual Metal Arc Welding

4) Thermit (Fusion) welding

Q 8) Which of these is a temporary joint?

1) Press fit joint

2) Welded joint

3) Brazed joint

4) Riveted joint

Q 9) Which of these is NOT a component of arc welding circuit?

1) Power source

2) Welding cable

3) Jig

4) Electrode holder with electrode

Q 10) As the length of the welding arc increases

1) The operating voltage increases

2) The operating voltage decreases

3) The operating voltage remains the same

4) The operating voltage may increase or decrease

INDUSTRIAL TRAINING INSTITUTE

Monthly Test-2, Marks- 20, Date:- ______________

(Every Question Carry Two Marks)

Q 11) Which of these is used to check shape and size of a weld bead?

1) Weld indicator

2) Weld template

3) Weld gauge

4) Weld dial

Q 12) Which of these machines converts AC into DC?

1) Amplifier

2) Inverter

3) Rectifier

4) Transformer

Q 13) The problem of arc blow is encountered when

1) Tranformer is used for welding

2) DC power supply is used for welding

3) When rectifier is used for welding

4) Any of the above is used

Q 14) In the figure of gas cutting torch shown below, which component controls flow of cutting oxygen?

1) Flow of cutting oxygen is controlled by A

2) Flow of cutting oxygen is controlled by B

3) Flow of cutting oxygen is controlled by C

4) Flow of cutting oxygen is controlled by D

Q 15) Electrical potential is also known by the name/ विद्यत ?मता को ________ नाम से

1) Electrical force

2) Electromotive force

3) Electrolytic force

4) Electromagnetic force

Q 16) Name the resistance welding process in which two wheels are used.

1) Silent butt welding
2) Flash butt welding
3) Seam welding
4) Projection welding
Q 17) In spot welding, electrodes are made of
2) Copper
3) Tungsten
4) Tin
Q 18) Which of these metals can be welded by TIG welding?
1) Copper
2) Aluminium
3) Stainless steel
4) All of these
Q 19) Which shielding gas is preferred for TIG welding of copper?
1) Argon
2) Helium
3) Mixture of argon and helium
4) Both argon and helium are equally good
Q 20) For TIG welding of aluminium, use of
1) DC with electrode positive gives better results
2) DC with electrode negative gives better results
3) AC gives better results
4) Any one of above will give good results

INDUSTRIAL TRAINING INSTITUTE

Monthly Test-3, Marks- 20, Date:- ______________

(Every Question Carry Two Marks)

Q 21) Which of these is NOT a high speed welding process?
1) Submerged arc welding
2) MIG welding
3) MAG welding
4) Gas welding
Q 22) What is NOT true about MIG welding process?
1) No slag is formed
2) No frequent change of electrode is required
3) Equipment required is expensive
4) Rate of metal deposition is slow
Q 23) Figure below shows gas cutting process. Kerf is indicated by
1) Kerf is indicated by A

2) Kerf is indicated by B
3) Kerf is indicated by C
4) Kerf is indicated by D
Q 24) Identify type of metal transfer in MIG welding as shown below
1) Dip transfer
2) Spray transfer
3) Globular transfer
4) None of these
Q 25) What is chemical formula of calcium carbide?
1) CaC
2) CaC2
3) Ca2C
4) Ca2C2
Q 26) Which of these is reducing agent or deoxidant?
1) Silicon
2) Manganese
3) Both of the above
4) None of these
Q 27) If a metal resists penetration, it is
1) Tough
2) Brittle
3) Hard
4) Ductile
Q 28) Figure below is simplified diagram of a transformer.
1) In it B indicated iron core
2) In it B indicates copper core
3) In it B indicates steel core
4) In it B indicates regulating core
Q 29) Why is cast iron preheated before welding?
1) To avoid shrinkage
2) To avoid cracking
3) To avoid hardening
4) To ensure all of the above
Q 30) In arc welding, closed butt joint is used on plated upto
1) 3 mm thick
2) 5 mm thick
3) 8 mm thick
4) 10 mm thick

INDUSTRIAL TRAINING INSTITUTE

Monthly Test-4, Marks- 20, Date:- _______________

(Every Question Carry Two Marks)

Q 31) The test which does not require use of electricity is

1) X - ray testing

2) Dye penetrant testing

3) Ultasonic testing

4) Hydraulic pressure testing

Q 32) What is arc time ?

1) The time the arc is on during the arc welding operation

2) The total time the worker is clocked into work

3) The non – arc time

4) The total arc and non – arc time

Q 33) Identify the joint shown below

1) Edge joint

2) Corner joint

3) Plug joint

4) Slot joint

Q 34) What is NOT correct about flux used in gas welding?

1) It is fusible

2) It is chemical compound

3) It dissolves oxides

4) None of these

Q 35) When gas welding, flux is not required for ......

1) Aluminium

2) Mild steel

3) Copper

4) Brass

Q 36) Visual examination of weld can help detect the defect

1) Undercut

2) Improper profile

3) Incomplete penetration

4) All of these

Q 37) What is the type of pipe joint shown in figure below?

1) Tee joint

2) Flange joint

3) Y joint

4) Branch joint

Q 38) The size of the cutting nozzle used in oxy-acetylene cutting depends mainly on

1) Thickness of the metal to be cut
2) Purity of oxygen
3) Duration of cut
4) Type of the cutting blowpipe

Q 39) How should the orifice of a blowpipe be cleaned?

1) Use soft steel wire
2) Use soft copper wire
3) Use tip cleaner
4) Use a small diameter drill

Q 40) The major part of atmospheric air is taken by

1) Oxygen
2) Nitrogen
3) Hydrogen
4) Argon

INDUSTRIAL TRAINING INSTITUTE

Monthly Test-5, Marks- 20, Date:- ______________

(Every Question Carry Two Marks)

Q 41) The letter H used as a suffix at the end of the electrode code indicates that it is ....

1) Heavy coated electrode
2) Low hydrogen electrode
3) Iron powder electrode
4) High tensile strength electrode

Q 42) Which test is done to find out percentage elongation of weldment?

1) Guided bend test
2) Tensile test
3) Fatigue test
4) Impact test

Q 43) Which welding defect can be easily detected by visual examination?

1) Lack of fusion
2) Misalignment of welded parts
3) Inter-bead slag inclusion
4) Root defect in T - fillet weld

Q 44) What will be the effect of long electrode stick-out in MIG / MAG welding

1) Excess weld metal
2) Low weld metal
3) Weld metal rough
4) Weld metal smooth

Q 45) Which inert gas will produce more stable arc in GMAW?
1) Argon
2) Helium
3) Carbon dioxide
4) All of these produce equally stable arc

Q 46) Which operating variable in submerged arc welding controls the arc length?
1) Welding speed
2) Welding voltage
3) Welding current
4) Electrode wire extension

Q 47) What is the size of gas nozzle for 1.5 mm diameter tungsten electrode in TIG welding process?
1) 10 mm diameter
2) 12 mm diameter
3) 14 mm diameter
4) 16 mm diameter

Q 48) Identify the weld defect in the bead shown in figure below.
1) Porosity
2) Slag inclusion
3) Lack of fusion
4) Lack of penetration

Q 49) One of the reasons for avoiding use of long arc in welding is ....
1) It gives lack of fusion in base metal
2) It increases open circuit voltage
3) It increases proability of crack in weld
4) It increases consumption of electrodes

Q 50) Application of which NDT does not require electricity?
1) X - ray test
2) Dye penetrant test
3) Ultrasonic test
4) Hydraulic pressure test

INDUSTRIAL TRAINING INSTITUTE

Monthly Test-6, Marks- 20, Date:- _______________

(Every Question Carry Two Marks)

Q 51) The principal advantage because of which iron powder electrodes are used, is ....

1) Time required to complete the weld is reduced
2) There will be no cracks in the weld
3) Flux coating becomes stronger
4) Resistance to flow of current is reduced

Q 52) Which statement is true about submerged arc welding?

1) vacuum Welding is done
2) Bare wire electrode is used
3) It can be applied for welding in any position
4) Rate of metal deposition is slow

Q 53) What is the advantage of using low heat input electrodes?

1) Very thin layer of weld metal can be applied
2) Distortion and warpage are reduced
3) Quality of weld metal is high
4) Surfacing can be done in all positions

Q 54) The welding symbol shown below is of ....

1) Square butt weld
2) Single - V butt weld
3) Double - V butt weld
4) Single - U butt weld

Q 55) What will be the effect of improper inert gas flow in TIG welding?

1) Porosity
2) Cracks
3) Lack of penetration
4) Weld metal getting oxidised

Q 56) Which electronic unit facilitates arc initiation in TIG welding?

1) Low frequency unit
2) Medium frequency unit
3) High frequency unit
4) Double frequency unit

Q 57) The nozzle used in TIG welding is made of ....

1) Bakelite
2) Ceramic
3) Plastic
4) Clay

Q 58) What will be defect if fusion does not take place up to root of the weld?

1) Blowholes

2) Lack of penetration

3) Porosity

4) Cracks

Q 59) Which non-destructive test can determine the depth of an internal weld defect?

1) Ultrasonic test

2) Magnetic particle test

3) Dye penetrant test

4) Eddy current test

Q 60) Which physical property helps to retain molten metal in position when welding is being done in overhead position?

1) Magnetic attraction

2) Surface tension

3) Capillarity

4) Thermal contraction

INDUSTRIAL TRAINING INSTITUTE

Monthly Test-7, Marks- 20, Date:- _______________

(Every Question Carry Two Marks)

Q 61) What is the shape of the tip of tungsten electrode used for TIG welding ofaluminium?

1) Pointed end

2) Flat end

3) Spherical end

4) Angular end

Q 62) Spot welding process basically depends upon ....

1) Application of forging pressure

2) Ohmic resistancc

3) Generation of heat

4) Generation of heat and application of forging pressure

Q 63) There are four modes of metal transfer in GMAW. Which one is considered least

desirable?

1) Spray

2) Pulsed spray

3) Globular

4) Short circuiting

Q 64) What type of electrodes are used in resistance seam welding?

1) Flat

2) Disc

3) Domed

4) Pointed

Q 65) Flux is required to be used in .... process.

1) TIG

2) MIG

3) MAG

4) SAW

Q 66) What is the preheat temperature to weld carbon steel pieces having 0.3% to 0.45% carbon?

1) 100 to120 C

2) 150 to 280 C

3) 280 to 350 C

4) 350 to 450 C

Q 67) Carbon supplied by the carburizing flame in gas welding makes the weld metal ....

1) Tough

2) Ductile

3) Brittle

4) Hard and brittle

Q 68) It is difficult to weld copper by resistance welding because of its ...

1) High thermal conductivity

2) High electrical conductivity

3) High toughness

4) High ductility

Q 69) What will happen if cast iron is welded without preheating?

1) Porosity

2) Undercut

3) Crack

4) Blowholes

Q 70) Which resistance welding machine is used to join pipe sections end-to-end?

1) Spot welding machine

2) Projection welding machine

3) Butt welding machine

4) Seam welding machine

INDUSTRIAL TRAINING INSTITUTE

Monthly Test-8, Marks- 20, Date:- _______________

(Every Question Carry Two Marks)

Q 71) What is the purpose of setting root gap (g in figure below) in a butt joint?

1) To obtain required depth of penetration

2) To control distortion

3) To maintain proper alignment

4) To deposit more metal

Q 72) Cast iron welding should be completed as quickly as possible. If slow welding is

done, it will cause burning of ....

1) Iron and phosphorus

2) Copper and iron

3) Carbon and silicon

4) Lead and phosphorus

Q 73) The type of joint used in spot welding is ....

1) Butt welding

2) Lap welding

3) Corner welding

4) Edge welding

Q 74) If three or more gas cylinders are connected together, the system is called ....

1) Portable system

2) Group system

3) Manifold system

4) High pressure system

Q 75) What may happen if a welder is arc welding while standing on wet floor?

1) Burn injury

2) Electric shock

3) Cut on the leg

4) Eye injury

Q 76) Which main factor will help cost of welding in a single V butt joint?

1) Weaving technique used

2) Correct included angle of V

3) Length of arc
4) Type of welding current used

Q 77) The zone next of the fusion zone in a welded joint is called ..
2) Adjacent zone
3) Heat-affected zone
4) Local zone

Q 78) Which of these metals has the highest thermal conductivity?
1) Mild steel
2) Copper
3) Aluminium
4) Zinc

Q 79) Oxy-acetylene cutting torch tip orifice should be cleaned with ....
1) Tip cleaner
2) Copper wire
3) Steel wire
4) Small size drill

Q 80) One of the reasons for avoiding the use of long arc in arc welding is ....
1) It will increase open circuit voltage
2) It will give lack of fusion of base metal
3) The joint will develop cracks
4) It will increase consumptionof electrodes

INDUSTRIAL TRAINING INSTITUTE

Monthly Test-9, Marks- 20, Date:- ______________

(Every Question Carry Two Marks)

Q 81) What will be the effect on distortion if the number of passes to complete a joint isincreased?
1) It will increase distortion
2) It will decrease distortion
3) It will have no effect on distortion
4) It will have very little effect on distortion

Q 82) Root bend test is used to test the amount of weld ....
1) Ductility
2) Elongation
3) Hardness
4) Penetration

Q 83) When water reacts with calcium carbide, the gas produced is ....

1) Hydrogen
2) Acetylene
3) Argon
4) Methane

Q 84) The circle used in a welding symbol means that welding is ....
1) To ensure that subsequent deposits are sound
2) To be all around the joint
3) To remove any excess flux
4) To relieve stresses in the first place

Q 85) In the iG position of pipe welding, the pipe must be ....
1) Rotated
2) Inclined
3) Horizontal
4) Vertical

Q 86) Which of these is a non-destructive test?
1) Nick break test
2) Impact test
3) Tensile test
4) Magnetic particle test

Q 87) The portion of the base metal that has not melted during welding but its microstructure has changed, is called _______
1) Fusion zone
2) Heat-affected zone
3) Dead zone
4) Twilight zone

Q 88) The heating of a welded joint immediately after having completed, it is called ..
1) Post heating
2) Delayed heating
3) Latc hcating
4) Fast heating

Q 89) Which of these welding processes requires the use of granular flux?
1) TIG welding
2) MIG welding
3) Submerged arc welding
4) Manual Metal Arc Welding

Q 90) What will happen if during TIG welding, tungsten electrode melts and deposits on weld metal?

1) Cracks will develop
2) There will be poor penetration
3) Weld metal will get contaminated
4) There will be lack of fusion

INDUSTRIAL TRAINING INSTITUTE

Monthly Test-10, Marks- 20, Date:- _______________

(Every Question Carry Two Marks)

Q 91) What can cause excessive burning of electrodes in arc welding?

1) Arc blow
2) Long arc length
3) Low quality electrodes
4) Too high welding current

Q 92) Which non-destructive test does not require supply from any power source?

1) X - ray test
2) Ultrasonic test
3) Dye penetrant test
4) Hydraulic pressure test

Q 93) What can happen if you see electric arc with naked eye?

1) Electric shock
2) Eye injury
3) Burn injury
4) Cut on legs and hands

Q 94) Which of these is one of the factors included in classification and coding of electrodes?

1) Type of flux coating
2) Length of electrode
3) Core diameter of electrode
4) Required baking temperature of electrode

Q 95) The property of a metal which enables it to stretch, bend or twist without cracking is called ....

1) Ductility
2) Malleability
3) Hardness
4) Toughness

Q 96) Which method of weld inspection is the cheapest?

1) Radiography
2) Ultrasonic test
3) Magnetic particle test
4) Visual examination

Q 97) What is the type of filler wire used in submerged arc welding?
1) Bare wire
2) Lightly coated wire
3) Heavily coated wired
4) Flux cored wire

Q 98) Which of these is an example of plastic welding?
1) Arc welding
2) Gas welding
3) Forge welding
4) Thermit welding

Q 99) Double V or double U edge preparation is normally used if the thickness of plates to be welded is ....
1) 1 - 5 mm
2) 5 - 10 mm
3) 10 - 15 mm
4) More than 15 mm

Q 100) The tip of a gas welding blowpipe is made of ....
1) Brass
2) Bronze
3) Copper
4) Mild steel

INDUSTRIAL TRAINING INSTITUTE

Monthly Test-11, Marks- 20, Date:- _______________

(Every Question Carry Two Marks)

Q 101) Which of these is a temporary joint?
1) Welded joint
2) Press fit joint
3) Brazed joint
4) Riveted joint

Q 102) What is the storage medium used to store acetylene gas in a cylinder at high pressure?
1) Petroleum jelly
2) Kerosene oil
3) Acetone

4) Water

Q 103) As a matter of safety never use .... on gas cylinders and regulators.

1) Wrench

2) Oil

3) Teflone tape

4) Leak detector

Q 104) Which oxy-acetylene flame contains excess of fuel gas?

1) Oxidising flame

2) Carburizing flame

3) Neutral flame

4) Standard flame

Q 105) Which is the most common (maximum percentage) gas in the atmosphere?

1) Oxygen

2) Nitrogen

3) Carbon dioxide

4) Methane

Q 106) An electric circuit is a path taken by flow of current. A path with no breaks is called ....

1) Closed circuit

2) Open circuit

3) Limited circuit

4) Continuous circuit

Q 107) Heat is measured in the units called ....

1) Newton

2) Joule

3) Watt

4) Celsius

Q 108) Always use .... to light a gas welding torch.

1) Matches

2) Striker

3) Electric arc

4) Cigarette lighter

Q 109) What term relates to amount of current flowing in an electric circuit?

1) Volt

2) Ampere

3) Ohm

4) Hertz

Q 110) What should be used to clean the tip of gas welding torch?

1) Steel wire

2) Copper wire

3) Copper coated steel wire

4) Tip cleaner

INDUSTRIAL TRAINING INSTITUTE

Monthly Test-12, Marks- 20, Date:- ______________

(Every Question Carry Two Marks)

Q 111) Which among the following has relatively the highest thermal conductivity?

1) Zinc

2) Mild steel

3) Copper

4) Aluminium

Q 112) In case of oxy-acetylene welding, oxygen cylinders are painted ....

1) White

2) Black

3) Maroon

4) Red

Q 113) Which gas welding flame is better suited to weld both ferrous and non-ferrous

metals?

1) Oxy-LPG flame

2) Oxy-acetylene flame

3) Oxy-hydrogen flame

4) Air-acetylene flame

Q 114) What is used to remove slag from a weld bead?

1) Mallet

2) Chipping hammer

3) Claw hammer

4) Sledge hammer

Q 1) The walls of welding shop should be painted

1) Dark colour

2) White colour

3) Reflecting colour

4) None of these

Q 2) For safety purpose, what is NOT good practice?

1) Use oil or grease on cylinder fittings

2) Keep cylinders cool

3) Not to use cylinders as rollers

4) Not to use cylinders as anvils

Q 3) What should be arc length in manual metal arc welding?

1) Approximately equal to electrode wire dia.

2) Approximately equal to half electrode wire dia.

3) Aproximately equal to double elecrode wire dia

4) Approximately equal to 1.5 times electrode wire dia.

Q 4) Which of these electrodes coating provides additional weld metal during welding?

1) Iron powder electrode

2) Mineral silicate

3) Calcium fluoride

4) Metal carbonate

Q 5) In dye penetrant test, the liquid dye is pulled out of the discontinuity by virtue of which action?

1) Heating

2) Cooling

3) Suction

4) Capillary

Q 6) Before fixing regulator on gas cylinder, the valve is opened a quarter turn and then closed immediately. What is this action called?

1) Checking

2) Setting

3) Testing

4) Cracking

9 798887 047584

Printed by Libri Plureos GmbH in Hamburg, Germany